DON'T GIVE UP THE SCRIPT!

Writing original sketches for the church

ROBERT A. ALLEN

MERIWETHER PUBLISHING LTD.
Colorado Springs, Colorado

Meriwether Publishing Ltd., Publisher
P.O. Box 7710
Colorado Springs, CO 80933

Editor: Rhonda Wray
Typesetting: Sharon E. Garlock
Cover design: Tom Myers

Library of Congress Cataloging-in-Publication Data

Allen, Robert A. (Robert Arthur), 1947-
     Don't give up the script : writing original sketches for the
church / by Robert Allen.
          p.   c.m.
     Includes bibliographical references. (p. 163).
     ISBN 1-56608-028-2 (pbk.)
     1. Drama in public worship--Authorship. 2. Christian drama--
Authorship. 3. Bible plays--Authorship.   I. Title.
     BV1534.4.A45   1996
     246'.72--dc21   96-47744
                                                                          CIP

1   2   3   4   5   6   7   8   9   99   98   97

This book is dedicated to my leading lady, Carmen, who played opposite my villain in our first stage experience and has graciously allowed me to act in a supporting role ever since.

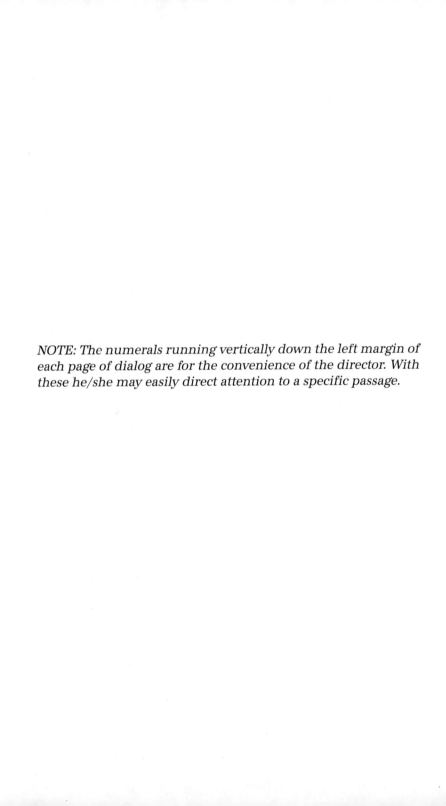

NOTE: The numerals running vertically down the left margin of each page of dialog are for the convenience of the director. With these he/she may easily direct attention to a specific passage.

CONTENTS

Preface vii

Introduction
18 ANGELS AND A ST. BERNARD 1

Chapter One
THE CHURCH AT PLAYS 9
(Drama in the Church)

Chapter Two
127 ACTORS AND A 15-FOOT STAGE 13
(Evaluating Resources)

Sketch: *The Importunate Friend* 21

Chapter Three
PLAY WITH A PURPOSE 27
(Choosing a Theme)

Sketch: *Variations on a Theme From Samson and Delilah* 31

Chapter Four
A FIGHT IN THE CHURCH 39
(Developing Conflict)

Sketch: *Guided Tour* 47

Chapter Five
**DID DANIEL REALLY WORRY ABOUT
SKIN BLEMISHES?** 55
(Developing Characters)

Sketch: *Patsy* 63

Chapter Six
ALL THE WORLD'S ON YOUR STAGE 69
(Planning Your Setting)

Sketch: *Heroes* 74

Chapter Seven
WORDS ARE FOR SPEAKING 77
(Writing Dialog)

Sketch: *Friendship Evangelism?* 85

Chapter Eight
GO AHEAD! WRITE IT DOWN! 89
(Preparing Your First Draft)

Assignment: *Developing Sketch Ideas* 93

Chapter Nine
GIVE IT A SKETCH-SHINE 107
(Revising)

Assignment: *Moses and the Rock* 111

Chapter Ten
IN SEARCH OF THE PERFECT FIT 117
(Tailoring Drama to Suit Your Needs)

Sketch Collection: *Introduction* 127

1. *First Church of Automation* 128

2. *First Church of Fame* 136

3. *First Church of Offense* 143

4. *First Church of Promotion* 148

5. *First Church of Reserve* 154

GLOSSARY OF STAGE TERMS 159

BIBLIOGRAPHY 163

ABOUT THE AUTHOR 165

PREFACE

Drama in the church has moved from an annual Christmas pageant to a regular Sunday morning occurrence as part of the worship service. Formerly relegated to the children, it has now been adopted by youth, adults and senior saints. Drama has been recognized as an effective evangelistic tool and a method of revitalizing worship. Pastors, worship leaders and congregations have recognized its value in bringing to life the truth of the Word of God and applying that truth to contemporary situations. Drama in the church has never been more alive than it is going into the twenty-first century.

Because of this rapid growth in the use of drama by the church, the need for dramatic sketches has also grown. Contemporary Drama Service, as well as other publishers, have sought to provide for that need. But many church drama directors, worship leaders and pastors find themselves faced with unique situations. They need sketches written specifically for their churches and their services. Many Christian dramatists are producing their own materials.

Don't Give Up the Script has been written to provide these dramatists with a valuable resource which will support and further their creative efforts. It is for all those who are regularly writing the words which others will be speaking on stage. Don't give up! Write those scripts! Determine to make every sketch and every line of dialog better than the one before. "My heart is indicting a good matter: I speak of the things which I have made touching the king: my tongue is the pen of a ready writer" (Psalm 45:1).

18 Angels and a St. Bernard

NOTE: *18 Angels and a St. Bernard* is not intended for production. It is designed to introduce the reader to the realities of discovering exactly the right script for performance. Although religious drama publishers continue to increase the availability of quality scripts, every director eventually faces that crisis moment known as "The-Perfect-Script-for-the-Present-Situation-Is-Not-Available" syndrome. It is from that moment until the time the stage curtain opens on your original drama that you need the constant encouragement — "DON'T GIVE UP THE SCRIPT."

CAST OF CHARACTERS

Harbinger Gloomp

In his late fifties, GLOOMP has been superintendent of the church school for almost a quarter of a century. During that time GLOOMP has perfected the art of arm-twisting, raising it almost to the level of inclusion in the church creed. He is best known for the time he rounded up seventeen substitute teachers during the time between the opening strains of "There's a Welcome Here" and the final chorus of "Happy Birthday to You." An eternal pessimist, the motto hanging over his desk reads, "If Anything Can Possibly Go Wrong, It Already Has." He wears a three-piece polyester suit even when mowing his lawn, which he does every Saturday afternoon whether it needs it or not. The way his Adam's apple bobs up and down over his tie reveals his desperate emotional state.

Serendipity Sue

SUE is one of GLOOMP's recruits. In high school she played the part of Laura in *The Glass Menagerie*. GLOOMP never saw the production, but one of the nursery workers heard about the play from her daughter and mentioned it to GLOOMP in passing. Since then SUE has directed every Christmas, Easter, Mother's Day, Promotion Day, Independence Day, Thanksgiving, Anniversary, All-Saints Day, Minister's Birthday, President's Day, New Years, Valentine's Day, Earth Day, Groundhog Day (you get the idea) Program ever presented by the church school. She has used scripts from every religious publisher in the nation (especially Contemporary Drama Service).

Scene: HARBINGER GLOOMP's office at the church school.

Time: The past, present or immediate future.

1   **Scene 1**

2

3   ***SETTING:*** HARBINGER GLOOMP's office is the second

4   door to the right and straight on toward mourning. He

5   shares his miniscule office with the church school's

6   multimedia resource center. Stacks of books provide

7   convenient seating while an overhead projector table

8   serves as a desk.

9   ***AT RISE:*** It is early evening. Seated on a stack of books,

10   HARBINGER GLOOMP pages through one of several

11   play catalogs piled at random on the top of the over-

12   head projector table. From a loudspeaker in the corner,

13   the faint strains of a practicing children's choir can be

14   heard. There is a knock on the door, and then

15   SERENDIPITY SUE sticks her head in.

16

17 **SUE: You wanted something, Mr. Gloomp?**

18 **GLOOMP:** *(Standing and waving at a pile of books)* **Come in**

19   **and sit down, Sue. We have to talk.**

20 **SUE:** *(She remains in the doorway.)* **Right now, Mr. Gloomp?**

21   **I'm in the middle of a rehearsal.**

22 **GLOOMP: Bad news! There's nothing available. Nothing!**

23   **Nothing! Nothing!**

24 **SUE: If I don't get back there soon, the children will be**

25   **finished singing and start climbing the walls.**

26 **GLOOMP: Walls? Are you doing Jericho for this program?**

27   **Never mind. We have to start thinking about the**

28   **next one.**

29 **SUE: The next one? Our opening performance is still a**

30   **week away.**

31 **GLOOMP: Can't afford to wait. If anything can possibly go**

32   **wrong...it already has.**

33 **SUE:** *(Finishing the line with him)* **...it already has. Shhh!**

34 **GLOOMP:** *(Listening to the speaker which is now silent)* **I**

1   **don't hear anything.**

2   **SUE: That's exactly what I was thinking. I've got to get back.**

3   **GLOOMP: But what are we going to do for the picnic?**

4   **SUE: Picnic?**

5   **GLOOMP: The picnic. I promised the church board that**
6   **all of the children would present a program at the**
7   **annual picnic in place of the three-legged race and**
8   **the pie toss. It seems some mothers had a difficult**
9   **time getting the peanut-butter yogurt pie out of their**
10   **children's clothes last year.**

11   **SUE:** *(With just a hint of sarcasm)* **So the church board**
12   **thought it would be much easier to put on a play**
13   **instead. Less work for the mothers and all.**

14   **GLOOMP: Exactly. I was thinking of something historical,**
15   **like a pageant on the origins of our church. It would**
16   **add a touch of authenticity if some of the children**
17   **could be cast in the role of their grandparents, don't**
18   **you think?**

19   **SUE: And you can't find anything like that in the play cata-**
20   **logs? Why am I not surprised?**

21   **GLOOMP:** *(With his Adam's apple bobbing)* **You've got to**
22   **help me, Sue. I'm desperate.** *(At this point there is a*
23   *crash over the speaker rivaling the fall of the Tower of*
24   *Babel, another play which is not in production at the*
25   *present time.)*

26   **SUE: So am I.** *(She disappears. Blackout)*

27

28   **Scene 2**

29

30   ***AT RISE:*** SERENDIPITY SUE is now seated on a stack of
31   books on the other side of HARBINGER GLOOMP's
32   projector table desk. One hour has passed and all the
33   children have gone home. Both SUE and GLOOMP are
34   leafing through catalogs.

1 SUE: Well, you're right. Not even Contemporary Drama
2 Service has a history play on the origin of our church.
3 I guess you'll just have to tell the church board to use
4 the feed bags from the gunny sack races to cover the
5 clothes of the children during the pie toss.
6 GLOOMP: Maybe a historical play was a bad idea. Just let
7 me tell you what we need and maybe you'll be able to
8 find a play that meets our needs.
9 SUE: Could we substitute a softball game?
10 GLOOMP: Softball is not acting.
11 SUE: Then why do they always talk about making a play at
12 home plate?
13 GLOOMP: You're testing my fruit of the Spirit, Sue.
14 SUE: Sorry, Mr. Gloomp. I wouldn't want to see your long-
15 suffering exhausted.
16 GLOOMP: The first requirement concerns space. We have
17 to present it out in the park.
18 SUE: No problem. Any play can be effective in the great
19 out-of-doors. Do you realize that Shakespeare was
20 originally performed in an open-air theatre between
21 London and China?
22 GLOOMP: How could he be between London and China?
23 SUE: Well, the theatre was just outside London and
24 the other side of the theatre was the other side of
25 the Globe.
26 GLOOMP: *(Stares at her with a puzzled look.)* What globe?
27 SUE: The Globe Theatre. It was called the Globe, see – oh,
28 forget it.
29 GLOOMP: In the park. And that means that none of the
30 young children can have any lines because we won't
31 have a microphone.
32 SUE: No lines for young children. But you still want them
33 on-stage, I presume.
34 GLOOMP: Right. Their parents will only be there to see

1   **them.**

2   **SUE: The telephone directory.**

3   **GLOOMP: The what?**

4   **SUE: We could use the telephone directory. Not much plot,**

5   **but a cast of thousands.**

6   **GLOOMP:** *(The puzzled expression returns.)* **The telephone**

7   **directory?**

8   **SUE: Forget it.**

9   **GLOOMP: All of the children must be used, including the**

10   **eighteen little angels from Mr. Webster's sixth-grade**

11   **class. He still hasn't forgotten the time you suggested**

12   **their class play be called "The Devils and Mr.**

13   **Webster."**

14   **SUE:** *(Shaking her head in resignation and despair. Now there's*

15   *a real challenge for an actress.)* **Eighteen little angels.**

16   **GLOOMP: And Hyram Schrempkrupper wants us to use**

17   **his St. Bernard dog. His name is Fluffy.**

18   **SUE: I thought you said it was Hyram. No, no. Forget**

19   **I said that. You can't be serious. No one is going to**

20   **publish a play that includes eighteen angels and a St.**

21   **Bernard dog.**

22   **GLOOMP: That's what I said. There's nothing! Nothing!**

23   **Nothing!**

24   **SUE: So we'll just have to tell the church board to try**

25   **human croquet. It worked well in *Alice in Wonder-***

26   ***land,* as I recall.**

27   **GLOOMP: Guess again.**

28   **SUE: *Alice Through the Looking-Glass?***

29   **GLOOMP: No, no, no. I mean we'll have to tell the board**

30   **that someone has decided to write a play.**

31   **SUE: Someone has decided to write a play?**

32   **GLOOMP: Right.**

33   **SUE: That's what I said, "write" a play.**

34   **GLOOMP: And I said – "right."**

1   SUE: **When you say "write," do you mean "write" as in,**
2   **"Someone has decided to write a play," or do you**
3   **mean "right" as in, "Right, someone has decided to**
4   **write a play"?**
5   GLOOMP: **I mean, you are going to write a play.**
6   SUE: *(With obvious sarcasm)* **I was afraid of that. Eighteen**
7   **angels, a St. Bernard dog, no lines for any of the cast,**
8   **a setting in the park and no peanut-butter yogurt pie**
9   **on the costumes. When do we get started?**
10 **GLOOMP:** *(Obviously missing the sarcasm)* **I knew you**
11 **would come through, Sue. We need the script**
12 **tomorrow.** *(She throws a peanut-butter yogurt pie in his*
13 *face. Blackout)*
14
15
16
17
18
19
20
21
22
23
24
25
26
27
28
29
30
31
32
33
34

CHAPTER ONE

The Church at Plays

Drama in the Church

Sixty years ago, Fred Eastman and Louis Wilson wrote a book called *Drama in the Church*. They introduced it by explaining "how to kill religious drama" — something which a few people would still love to do today. Their suggestions for "killing" religious drama included wishing it upon the children, turning it over to the choir director or some "nice young girl who once had a part in a high school play," providing no equipment, using only nonroyalty plays and following the play "with a sermon pointing out the moral and urging greater gifts to the church" (Willett, Clark and Co., 1933).

Since that time drama in the church has grown from infancy to adolescence, gaining acceptance by many congregations, yet still not accorded adult status when compared to other forms of ministry, service and worship. Adolescence, however, is a period of rapid growth and a growth spurt vividly describes the last few years of religious drama. Once confined to the annual, obligatory Christmas program, drama now thrives on many different days of the church year.

Willow Creek Community Church in Barrington, Illinois, has used drama successfully for many years in its Son City youth ministry. They are known across the country for their sketch performances as part of the worship experience. Steve Pederson, Willow Creek's Drama Director, explains the philosophy of his ministry in a letter addressed to those who have shown an interest in participating:

> Let me briefly explain our philosophy concerning drama here at Willow Creek. First of all, the sketches are written to coincide with a message. Because the drama and message are presented as a package, we try to avoid "preaching' in the sketches.

9

Rather, we attempt to creatively approach an issue by presenting contemporary characters, with whom our audience can identify. We resist resorting to easy answers or simple platitudes. A number of our sketches are not "Christian" in and of themselves, but they are tied thematically to a biblical message. The sketches are also written in an attempt to communicate to the nonchurched.

Pederson goes on to say that, "while the sketches appear fairly simple and direct, they are actually deceptively difficult to write." He explains that "the biggest challenge we face is developing the scripts." He cautions those who would like to start a drama ministry in their church that "beginning a drama group with the purpose of performing regularly in your church is not an easy task." But he also encourages them. "Many churches across the country have caught on to how valuable a communication tool drama can be and have been able to successfully implement it regularly."

Wooddale Church of Minneapolis sometimes uses short dramas as part of their worship service. Pastor Leith Anderson formed a committee of five to write sketches corresponding with the themes of his messages. Their goal was to write sketches four to five minutes long which would become an integral part of the service, just like the choir anthem or the Scripture reading. They kept production details to a minimum, so they could be performed on the platform with a minimum of equipment. Their approach was to deal with Bible stories as if they were taking place today, giving them a contemporary flavor.

During a series on the fruit of the spirit, the drama committee wrote a skit to illustrate each fruit as Pastor Anderson preached on it. For the message on kindness, they introduced a wife anxiously awaiting the arrival of her husband. He had been in a motorcycle accident and explained that the only person who had stopped to help him was a member of the Hell's Angels. This bearded, leather-jacketed cyclist had taken him to the hospital and even paid his bill. When the husband asked his name, he simply replied, "You can call me Sam."

When the committee developed a sketch around the story of Ruth, they had Naomi moving from Minneapolis back to Brainerd, Minnesota, to be among her own people. The story of the temptation of Joseph took place in a health spa.

Pastor Anderson is also known for his costumed monologs of Bible characters such as Noah and Adam, which sometime take the place of an entire message.

Not every church uses the method of short sketches tied in with the theme of the message. Pasadena First Church of the Nazarene, for example, presents full-length dramas like *Bonhoeffer: Who Stands Fast?*. This play was directed by Artist-in-Residence James Bradford.

Hundreds of other churches are using drama as well in many and varied ways. St. Paul's Drama Guild of Kansas City is involved in dinner theatre. Bethesda Baptist Church of Brownsburg, Indiana, took one of their plays into the Indiana Women's Prison. First Baptist drama group of San Angelo, Texas, toured with an original musical play. The Master Arts Company of Grand Rapids, Michigan, presented a dramatic reading of *The Book of Job.*

Another ministry to local churches takes place through the drama teams which tour from Christian colleges and universities. These troupes of drama students prepare sketches, one-acts and full-length dramas and present them on weekends throughout the school year or on longer tours during vacation periods. Churches which don't have a regular drama ministry can be introduced to drama in the church in this manner. Several churches, after seeing the Pillsbury Players from Pillsbury Baptist Bible College in Owatonna, Minnesota, perform, have been encouraged to use drama in their own congregations as well.

So drama in the church is becoming more common during this period of dramatic adolescence. "But it is generally a bit of an uphill battle," says Willow Creek's Steve Pederson, "because drama in church is unusual, especially on a weekly or even monthly basis."

There are also a few professional ensembles of theatre artists who perform both inside and outside the church. Among these are the Lamb's Players of National City, California, the A. D. Players of Houston, Texas, the Covenant Players of Oxnard, California, and the Jeremiah People of Los Angeles.

One of the greatest signs of the vitality of church drama is the increasing availability of scripts designed specifically for a variety of religious experiences. But there are still many events in the church year which call for a specific dramatic message which you can't find in the catalogs. For this reason, it is helpful to list events in every month of the church calendar which could be celebrated through the use of drama. The possibilities include: youth plays, family nights, spontaneous drama and hotchpotch plays, clown skits, revues, dinner theatre, historical drama and more.

Those who seek to correlate drama with a series of sermon themes quickly discover that they must try their hand at writing their own scripts. As Steve Pederson said, "The biggest challenge we face is developing the scripts." That's great! Use all the tremendous sketches which have become available, and when the occasion calls for it — write your own.

CHAPTER TWO

127 Actors and a 15-Foot Stage

Evaluating Resources

The acting troupe from a small church in Montana had been on tour for a week with a musical called *The Frumious Bandersnatch.* Now in Minnesota and preparing for their eighth performance, they thought they had faced every staging situation possible. But they were wrong.

This church met in an old stone edifice, stately on the outside and appropriately somber and full of worshipful atmosphere within. But the stage was a director's nightmare. Built on three different levels to accommodate a pulpit, choir loft and access area, the entire platform was still not more than fifteen feet wide. To complicate matters further, each area had been defined by permanent, three-foot polished oak walls through which tiny gates allowed one person at a time to squeeze through to get from place to place. One of the main characters in the musical, a fuzzy playground toy who comes to life, had a side-to-side girth of four feet himself.

The entire play had to be re-blocked between supper and the 7:00 p.m. performance.

Unless your church auditorium was constructed specifically with drama in mind, you probably will not have an ideal situation for play production, although hopefully it will not generate the nightmares faced by those young people from Montana. An important lesson every writer and director learns early in the dramatic experience is how to make the best possible use of the resources available.

The encouraging word for writers is that plays have been performed in every possible environment from garages to parks to gymnasiums. Drama will work in your church auditorium, no matter how it is constructed.

All the World's a Stage?

Most stages are constructed in a manner somewhat similar to a church with a raised platform at one end of a rectangular hall. The biggest difference would be that in a theatre, a large arch called the "proscenium" sets the platform off from the rest of the building. The opening created by the proscenium contains a curtain which may be drawn or lowered to mask or reveal the acting area. Churches seldom have such a proscenium, preferring instead an open architecture where the platform is always in view of the audience.

The proscenium stage is not the only one used by theatres. The Guthrie Theatre in Minneapolis and others have built a "thrust" stage where the acting platform extends out into the audience. Seats surround it on three sides. This can be a very effective style of architecture for a church as well, because it has the effect of bringing a speaker much closer to those who are listening.

The "arena" stage will probably not be found in a church situation. Used for theatre-in-the-round, this platform is set in the middle of the room, surrounded on every side by audience. Entrances and exits are made through the aisles. Plays are not usually written specifically for the arena stage, but most plays can be adapted to this type of environment.

Evaluation Time

As you begin developing the ideas for your script, take a close look at the area where it will eventually come to life. What entrances and exits are available? Will it be possible to extend the size of the platform by adding risers at the front? Can the pews in the choir loft be removed to provide additional space? Are platform fixtures permanent or will it be possible to remove them? Can they be removed quickly and then restored if the sketch is to be part of a larger worship context?

The answers to these questions will affect the play — particularly in the area of spectacle. A patriotic script which calls for 127 children to march eight abreast across the stage waving flags and singing *The Battle Hymn of the Republic* probably wouldn't work on a fifteen-foot stage. By the time the last eight were ready to make their entrance, the first eighty-seven would be out on the playground re-enacting the Civil War.

Spectacle is the element which sets drama apart from other literary forms. Although a play can be read and enjoyed, its ultimate purpose is achieved by production. That production involves space and time, actors and audience. The playwright does not just compose dialog, he also designs action which brings to life the thoughts and character of the people portrayed. Effective drama will be both verbal and visual. The visualization of the scene requires space through which the actors will move.

Close your eyes and see the scene you are creating in the space where it will eventually be performed. Does the space allow for the actions you have planned? Can the actors make the entrances and exits called for? Is there room for the entire Sunday school to be present on the platform at the same time? If that is necessary, could they provide a background against which the visual action could take place?

With space considerations in mind, a sketch to be used as a part of a Sunday worship service should probably call for a minimum of spectacle. Elaborate backdrops, box sets, fog machines and scrims should be reserved for Christmas and Easter pageants. Plan to write your sketches for the existing space at the front of your auditorium. A desk could suffice to suggest the reception room in a doctor's office. A single chair could represent a living room. A park bench could transport your entire audience to an outdoor setting. Don't be limited by your acting space. Instead, remove all limitations by using your imagination and challenging the audience to do the same.

In addition to evaluating the stage, the writer also needs to consider time requirements. The traditional full-length play which runs approximately two hours will not normally be a part of the church service experience. One-act plays up to one hour in length have been used effectively when a church wishes to devote an entire service to a dramatization of the message.

The most common use of drama in the church, however, has become the short play, four to ten minutes long, which blends into a larger theme and prepares the congregation for the preaching in the same manner as the Scripture reading, choir number or congregational singing. This is the play form which has become known as the sketch.

Skits or Sketches?

In Debra Poling and Sharon Sherbondy's book *Super Sketches for Youth Ministry* (Zondervan), they make a strong point of differentiating between skits and sketches. Skits have been used in summer camps and with youth groups for years with the purpose of "allowing anyone in your youth group to let loose, have fun, get attention, and make others laugh." The typical skit ends with someone either sitting in a pan of water, being hit in the face with a cream pie or making a fool of himself in some other equally hilarious way (if you are not on the receiving end). Junior high camp would not be complete without a skit night.

Sketches, however, "are for communicating life truths. All those other fun things may happen, but with a sketch, the point is to make a point." A sketch should be like a full-length play in its construction, but like a very short one-act play in its length. It should have a beginning, conflict, crisis and resolution. Poling and Sherbondy add that sketches should be "taken seriously," they should draw in the audience emotionally and they should have "the potential to change lives."

The sketch writer must know what time limits are faced before undertaking the task of writing a script. Meet with your pastor and other worship leaders and find out from them exactly what time will be allowed for a dramatic sketch in the service. Then write and rehearse to meet that time limit precisely. There are few circumstances which frustrate a pastor more than to find it necessary to cut his message short because earlier participants in the service took more than their allotted time. Since the purpose of your sketch is to enhance the message, you certainly don't want to decrease the effectiveness of the entire thematic package by taking time away from the very element of the service you are seeking to support.

Calling All Actors

Another resource which must be evaluated is your actors. A well-written script can be ruined or greatly enhanced by those who assume the roles it creates. If you have a group in the church already organized and trained, it would be good to keep the abilities of these individuals in mind while writing. At the same time, if you have available persons with some experience in acting, you will want to produce scripts which will continue to challenge them to develop their talent.

Willow Creek Community Church's drama minister, Steve Pederson, recommends auditions as a method for finding actors. But he also says, "Don't be afraid to personally invite some who show potential." Sometimes people who like to show off are seen by others as good actors, but often your best actors will be those who can appear natural on-stage, rather than artificial or "hammy."

In one sense, a writer does not write the "acting" which takes place on-stage. That is developed by the individual actors working with a director. But the writer does come up with the idea of the action of the sketch, he describes the characters doing the action and he provides the words those characters will speak. This produces a co-dependency in drama. The actor depends on the writer to describe an action, and the writer depends on the actor to enliven that action. One of the best preparations any writer can make is to get on-stage and experience what it is like to bring someone's characters to life. If you have never acted, then by all means get on-stage before trying to write for the stage.

The playwright must write sketches for actors. Even the most talented actor will not be able to bring to life the character a writer conceives unless he understands and feels what that character is like. An incomprehensible script will not be made clear simply by reading it aloud. The script itself must reveal the character in such a way that the actor can understand the thoughts, emotions, words and actions of that character. The actor will then combine those with his own personality. These clues to the subject's thoughts, emotions and actions will be revealed in the stage directions, in the character's own dialog and also in what other characters say about him or her.

In order to make your sketch one which can easily be acted rather than just performed, you must have specific actors in mind as you write. They don't need to be people you know, but they must be people you can visualize. For them, you will write appropriate and easily articulated diction. If you hear them stumbling over your word construction, rewrite so the words can be spoken with ease. For them, you will write dialog which in its very word choice helps to reveal character. For them, you will develop an intensity of emotion which will stimulate them to physical action on-stage.

If you are working with the same group of actors week after week, you will have a tremendous advantage in that you will be familiar with their abilities, and therefore you will be able to envision your sketch being performed as you write.

On-Stage Action

Three terms are used to describe the action which takes place on-stage. Blocking is the movement of the actors from place to place on the stage. It includes entrances and exits but, beyond those, the writer usually leaves the blocking up to the actor and the director. The physical arrangement of the stage will be the important factor in determining the blocking.

"Business" is another word for gesture, the small movements that reveal character. Meaningful movements of the face, hands, feet and body belong in this category. How the character stands and sits and walks or executes social movements such as bowing or shaking hands would be considered business, as are the handling of props or costume pieces, such as a sword or fan. Some of these matters of business will be included by the writer in the script, but again, many of them will be developed by the actor as he develops his role.

Peripheral movements include all other physical activities of the actors. Actors who are comfortable on-stage will even scratch their ears and blink their eyes in a manner which helps to reveal character. Those who are uncomfortable will discover that it is peripheral movement which makes them appear nervous and unprofessional. The writer who provides an actor with specific actions which further the plot and develop character will help the actor feel at ease, because she will know what should be done with both business and peripheral movements.

Working the Crowd

As the script writer evaluates resources, it is important to consider the audience. What are the expectations of those who will be viewing the sketch? Will they expect to be entertained, or will they be surprised to discover humor in a worship situation? Will they be willing to separate the actors as characters from the actors as people they know off-stage?

As a writer, you must know the theological background of your audience. Would your church be considered conservative or liberal, mainline or evangelical, charismatic or noncharismatic? Is it more liturgical or free form in its worship patterns? Will the congregation viewing your sketch be mainly adults, or will teenagers and children be present? Will unchurched persons be in attendance? Is the potential audience predominantly high-, middle- or low-income? Executives, housewives or retirees? You must constantly evaluate the effect your sketch will have on those who are listening. Remember, a sketch should make a point and have the potential for changing lives.

The audience is one of the most important resources for the writer. When Eugene O'Neill's play *Dynamo* bombed in its initial performances, O'Neill admitted that it had not been ready for production because he neglected to sit through rehearsals and listen to the performance from the viewpoint of the audience. Later, while attending the first few performances of *Strange Interlude*, he kept cutting lines from the play. When one of the actors complained that he was cutting out the big laughs, O'Neill replied, "That is exactly what I want to do. A laugh relieves the tension. I want to build as much tension as possible in the audience, and that is the reason for removing any tendency to laugh at this point."

19

Learn to listen to rehearsals from the standpoint of the audience. Ask yourself, "How would my grandmother react to this?" Or, "What would these words suggest to a single mother?" Or sit in the middle of the audience during the performance of your sketch and honestly evaluate the reactions around you.

Audiences will also differ in the amount of Bible knowledge they bring to the dramatic experience. Many churches who use drama in "seeker" services deliberately limit the theological language of the plays they use. The purpose of the drama in that situation is to focus the attention of the audience on a problem which will later be addressed in a sermon. The congregation in another church may have years of experience in understanding the language of the Bible. The writer must know the potential audience because the audience will always be the final judge of the effectiveness of the sketch you write.

The following sketch has seen over one hundred tour performances on every imaginable stage, from gymnasium floors to a crowded cubicle in South Africa. Its versatility makes it a good example of a sketch which may be adapted to fit the resources of any acting troupe. The sketch first appeared in *The Youth Leader* and is reprinted by permission.

The Importunate Friend

Based on Luke 11:5-10

by Robert A. Allen

"A friend of mine has come on a journey,
and I have nothing to feed him."

CAST OF CHARACTERS

Director

Neighbor

Friend

Friend's Wife

Neighbor's Wife

Traveler

PRODUCTION NOTES

Two stools at Stage Right represent the Neighbor's house. The Neighbor and the Neighbor's Wife sit there with their backs to the audience when they are asleep and turn around to the front when awakened. There is no other furniture on-stage. Characters can be costumed in modern dress or in robes and sandals from the New Testament period. The Director should be in modern costume in either case.

1   **DIRECTOR: All right, let's have it quiet. Quiet on the set.**
2   **Today we're going to tell the story of the importunate**
3   **friend.**
4   **NEIGHBOR:** *(Interrupting)* **You mean the important friend?**
5   **DIRECTOR: That's what I said, the importunate friend.**
6   **NEIGHBOR: But that's not what I said. I said important.**
7   **It's the important friend.**
8   **DIRECTOR: Who's directing this play anyway, you or me?**
9   **NEIGHBOR: Well, you are, of course. The script gives all**
10   **your lines to the Director.**
11   **DIRECTOR: So?**
12   **NEIGHBOR: So?**
13   **DIRECTOR: So, it's like I said. The importunate friend.**
14   **NEIGHBOR: But importunate doesn't mean anything.**
15   **DIRECTOR: Yes, it does.**
16   **NEIGHBOR: All right, what does it mean?**
17   **DIRECTOR: Well, importunate means...it means...all**
18   **right, you win. It's the important friend.**
19   **FRIEND: Wait a minute. I didn't try out for this play to**
20   **be the important friend. I'm supposed to be the**
21   ***importunate* friend.**
22   **DIRECTOR:** *(Stage whisper)* **So what does it mean? How**
23   **can I be the director if I don't know what it means?**
24   **FRIEND:** *(Stage whisper)* **I'll tell you, and you tell him, OK?**
25   **DIRECTOR: OK.**
26   **FRIEND:** *(Stage whisper)* **The importunate friend...**
27   **DIRECTOR:** *(Loudly to NEIGHBOR)* **The importunate friend.**
28   **FRIEND:** *(Stage whisper)* **...is a friend who asks for a**
29   **favor....**
30   **DIRECTOR:** *(Loudly and dramatically)* **...is a friend who**
31   **asks for a favor....**
32   **FRIEND:** *(Stage whisper)* **Don't overdo it.**
33   **DIRECTOR:** *(Loudly)* **Don't overdo it.**
34   **FRIEND:** *(Groans and then continues in a stage whisper.)*

22

1   …and won't quit asking, even when turned down.
2   **DIRECTOR:** *(Loudly)* **…and won't quit asking, even when**
3   **turned down.**
4   **NEIGHBOR: Well, it still sounds to me like he thought he**
5   **was pretty *important*.**
6   **FRIEND:** *(Arguing with NEIGHBOR)* **Importunate!**
7   **NEIGHBOR:** *(To FRIEND)* **Important!**
8   **DIRECTOR:** *(Shouting)* **Quiet! Quiet on the set. Let's get**
9   **busy here. Neighbor, these stools are your house. It's**
10   **midnight, and you and your wife are asleep.**
11   *(NEIGHBOR and NEIGHBOR'S WIFE take their places on*
12   *the stools. FRIEND, FRIEND'S WIFE and TRAVELER*
13   *exit.)* **Friend, you come over to your neighbor's house**
14   **from where you live next door. Now, let's be very**
15   **careful to say our lines distinctly. I want everyone to**
16   **enunciate.** *(Shouting)* **Enunciate!** *(The first time*
17   *through, each character speaks slowly, with over-precise*
18   *enunciation, but in a monotone.)*
19   **FRIEND: Neighbor! Neighbor Brown. Wake up. Wake up.**
20   **NEIGHBOR: What is it? What do you want at this time of**
21   **night?**
22   **FRIEND: I need you to lend me three loaves of bread.**
23   **NEIGHBOR: Three loaves of bread at midnight?**
24   **FRIEND: Yes, three loaves.**
25   **NEIGHBOR: Why three loaves of bread at midnight?**
26   **FRIEND: A friend of mine has come on a journey, and I**
27   **have nothing to feed him.**
28   **NEIGHBOR: But I'm already in bed.**
29   **FRIEND: Already in bed? I need three loaves.**
30   **NEIGHBOR: And my wife has already gone to bed.**
31   **FRIEND: But I need three loaves of bread.**
32   **NEIGHBOR: My children are already asleep. You'll wake**
33   **them.**
34   **FRIEND: But I need three loaves.**

1   **NEIGHBOR'S WIFE: What is all the ruckus? Who's out**
2   **there?**
3   **NEIGHBOR: It's our friend. He needs three loaves of**
4   **bread.**
5   **NEIGHBOR'S WIFE: Three loaves of bread?**
6   **FRIEND: To feed a hungry traveler.**
7   **NEIGHBOR'S WIFE: A hungry traveler?** *(FRIEND'S WIFE*
8   *enters.)*
9   **FRIEND'S WIFE: Honey, do you have the bread yet?**
10   **NEIGHBOR: Who's out there now?**
11   **FRIEND: My wife. Please give us the bread.**
12   **NEIGHBOR: But it's midnight.** *(TRAVELER enters.)*
13   **TRAVELER: Oh, I'm so hungry. I think I'll die if I don't**
14   **have some bread.**
15   **FRIEND'S WIFE: Give us the bread.**
16   **FRIEND: Can't you see how much we need it?**
17   **NEIGHBOR'S WIFE: Give them the bread, dear.**
18   **TRAVELER: Bread! Bread!**
19   **DIRECTOR:** *(Shouting)* **Cut! Cut!**
20   **TRAVELER: I don't care if it's cut or not. Just give me the**
21   **bread.**
22   **NEIGHBOR: All right. Here's the bread.**
23   **DIRECTOR: No! I mean cut! Quit! Stop! This is terrible.**
24   **This story is filled with emotion. We need to have**
25   **some emotion. You're all dead. Liven it up a little.**
26   **Show us some tears.**
27   *(The entire script is repeated from the entrance of the*
28   *friend. This time the cast uses exaggerated emotion.*
29   *Tears flow freely. The DIRECTOR's last line and transi-*
30   *tion into the next part follows.)*
31
32   **DIRECTOR: No! I mean cut! Quit! Stop! This is terrible.**
33   **Remember, the story has a happy ending. We need to**
34   **have a little touch of humor. Come on, let's do it again**

1   **with some humor. All right. Take three!**

2   *(The entire script is repeated from the entrance of the*

3   *friend. This time the cast laughs at every line. The*

4   *DIRECTOR's last line and transition into the ending*

5   *follows.)*

6

7   **DIRECTOR: No! I mean cut! Quit! Stop! This is terrible.**

8   **What is the point of continuing on? What is the point?**

9   **CAST:** *(Unison)* **The point is...**

10   **NEIGHBOR: Though he will not rise and give him,**

11   **because he is his friend, yet because of his importu-**

12   **nity he will rise and give him as many as he needeth.**

13   **FRIEND: Ask and it shall be given unto you; seek and ye**

14   **shall find; knock and it shall be opened unto you.**

15   **CAST:** *(Unison)* **For every one that asketh receiveth, and he**

16   **that seeketh findeth; and to him that knocketh it**

17   **shall be opened** (Luke 11:8-10).

18

19

20

21

22

23

24

25

26

27

28

29

30

31

32

33

34

CHAPTER THREE

Play With a Purpose

Choosing a Theme

Drama in the church should always have a purpose, and that purpose should go beyond entertainment. Even though there is nothing wrong with laughter in church, sketches should do more than just add a few minutes of humor to a person's day. We have a message to communicate which happens to be the greatest message ever announced to mankind. Our goal as writers should be to communicate that message to an audience by means of one of the greatest methods of communication ever devised — the drama.

This purpose which every sketch must contain is called the theme. It is not the same as the story or plot line. A pastor may take the story of David and Goliath in I Samuel 17 as a text and develop numerous messages from that passage depending on the theme he chooses to explore. He could bring a message on the theme: "Depending on God turns certain defeat into victory." Or he could approach the story from the viewpoint of the army and explore this idea: "Doubting God makes us servants to the things we fear." He could look at the relationship between David and his brothers and choose the theme: "Jealousy robs families of the opportunity to work together in overcoming problems." All of these are themes drawn from the same story.

Variety in theme makes it possible for a pastor to use the same text or portion of Scripture and draw from that passage several messages. Used correctly, it keeps preaching fresh — even when a man stays in the same pulpit for many years. It also makes it possible for many writers to draw from the same source, the Bible, and write a great variety of sketches illustrating different themes.

A well-written theme is also what keeps a sermon vital and makes it practical for the listener. It takes familiar biblical material and looks at it from a viewpoint unfamiliar to the audience. The truth, presented from that new viewpoint, causes people to think and possibly even brings conviction.

The theme is the point you are trying to make by telling your story. It expresses a point of view chosen by the writer, a particular way in which he chooses to tell the story in order to impress a message upon the audience. The playwright who does not have a theme may provide an audience with entertainment, but he will not leave them with something to think about. One of the great advantages of using comedy in religious drama is that it makes people think about themes which they would otherwise avoid if they were not laughing about the story.

The theme does not determine whether the sketch will take a serious or light approach. The same theme could be treated in either fashion. "Family accepts us with all our faults" could be the theme for a tragedy concerning a family who learns to love a child with a drug problem. But it could also be the theme for a comedy where a boy who makes a fool of himself on his first date finds in his family those who can laugh with him about his actions.

Sometimes the theme of a passage of Scripture is clearly stated, as in the case of the parables which Jesus loved to use in his teaching. *The Importunate Friend* (page 21) was based on Christ's parable in Luke 11:5-10. It takes its theme directly from the explanation which Christ included: People should be persistent in prayer. The theme surfaces throughout the sketch in several different ways. The story line shows how the neighbor was willing to approach his friend even after midnight and keep asking for bread until he received it. During the sketch, the entire story is repeated three times, which illustrates the theme of persistence. At the end of the sketch, the theme is stated directly as the words of Christ's explanation are used in response to the frustrated cry of the director, "What's the point?"

During one production of this sketch, a small girl was seen leaving the auditorium. When her teacher stopped her, she said, "I know there's some bread down in the kitchen. I'm going to go get some for them." Not every person in an audience will be moved to such immediate action by your theme, but it should be there so they can take it with them and perhaps allow it to influence their lives at some later date.

When in Doubt – Write It Out

Writing down a clear theme before you begin work on your sketch will help you to focus direction. If you fail to choose a theme, you may get to the end of your writing and ask yourself, like the director in *The Importunate Friend,* "What's the point?" As soon as you get an idea of the story you want to tell, write your theme as a complete sentence.

The subject of the sentence should be the concept *you*, the playwright, are discussing, rather than one of the characters in the sketch. This will assure you of a contemporary message even when dealing with historical subjects. Sometimes you hear sermons which make this mistake. The preacher explains how David trusted God in his defeat of Goliath but leaves the audience thinking, "That was fine for David, but how is it relevant to me?"

The verb in your sentence should be active. The stronger the action verb, the more options you will have for creating action in the story line. Avoid state-of-being verbs completely. The theme "Doubt is a great problem" doesn't go anywhere. It is completely static. The theme "Doubt makes us servants to the things we fear" suggests action. You can visualize a fear making someone into a servant.

Finally, your sentence should have an object. What will be the result of the action you describe? "Pride leads the way to destruction." "Envy rots the core of a relationship." "Greed destroys the harmony of a happy family." Each of these themes could be applied to familiar Bible stories, and each would make a strong point if used as the basis for a sketch.

Theme Ideas

Here is a list of themes which could provide the basis for one of the sketches you are going to write. As you read through the list, try to match each theme with a Bible story which could be the basis for a contemporary sketch illustrating that theme.

Evil companions corrupt behavior.

Genuine compassion demands action.

Charity benefits both giver and receiver.

Wrong choices result in lost opportunities.

Evangelism requires personal involvement.

Failure can prepare us for success.

Victory guarantees greater trials.

Grace provokes us to graciousness.

Healing begins when sickness is acknowledged.

Faith astonishes the unfaithful.

Thanks belongs to the Giver and not the gift.

Neighborliness reveals a godly heart.

Gossip thrives in hypocritical prayers.

Service expects no service itself.

Pride goeth before destruction.

Christian liberty requires Christian grace.

Friendly enemies hide wicked motives.

The theme "Even the strongest need God" runs through the story of Samson and Delilah. Notice how it can be emphasized in a humorous fashion while challenging actors in the use of various dramatic styles. Then see how many other themes you can discover in the same story.

Variations on a Theme From Samson and Delilah

by Robert A. Allen

"Oh, I love the story of Samson and Delilah.
It's so romantic."

CAST OF CHARACTERS

Clint

Chad

Casey

Joe

Melissa

Wendy

Bonni

Colleen

PRODUCTION NOTES

The play takes place on a stage that is bare except for a chair in the front of a church auditorium.

The only required props are six pieces of poster board with one letter each, spelling S-A-M-S-O-N.

1   CLINT: All right, let's get to work. You all know that Pastor
2   will be preaching on Samson and Delilah this coming
3   Sunday and he wants us to present a dramatic lead-in
4   to the message.
5   COLLEEN: Oh, I love that story. It's so romantic.
6   JOE: Kind of hairy, if you ask me.
7   MELISSA: I think Casey should play Samson to my Delilah.
8   BONNI: I thought Samson had muscles.
9   CLINT: Hey, cut it out. We need to get serious here.
10 CHAD: My sentiments exactly. I perceive the story of
11   Samson and Delilah as containing all of the essential
12   elements of Greek Tragedy. Their characters stride
13   the stage with such immortals as Oedipus,
14   Agamemnon and Antigone.
15 WENDY: Too bad we don't have a Sophocles or Euripides
16   around to write us a script.
17 CASEY: Euripides? Wasn't he the guy who tore his pants
18   and took them to the tailor. "Euripides?" says the
19   tailor. "Right! Eumenides?" *(All groan.)*
20 CLINT: OK, enough of that. Let's see how Samson and
21   Delilah would work in the style of Greek Tragedy. *(All*
22   *gather into a group as the Greek chorus from which indi-*
23   *vidual characters will emerge.)*
24 CHORUS: Forty years since, the great Jehovah,
25   implored by Manoah, from Danite heritage
26   of Zorah born,
27   whose wife had barren lived,
28   as eagle cries from rocky crag
29   pierce heart of prey lost far below,
30   responded he with message kind.
31 ALL MEN: "Conceive you will and bear a son."
32 CHORUS: With warning clear did Samson come,
33   received with threefold message,
34   eat not unclean,

32

1   unwined remain,
2   unrazored head from womb till dead.
3   Now twenty years
4   away from Dan
5   through Timnath lion, Etam rock,
6   fox's tail and donkey's jaw,
7   Ramath-lehi, En-hakkore,
8   Gaza, Ashkelon,
9   Philistine thousands fall,
10   leaf withered to their long home flee
11   before the arm of Hercules
12   the judge, the hero, Samson.
13   But you, oh Samson,
14   In persuasion of what report appear you now?
15   CHAD: From beacon fire to beacon fire
16   the cedar flames like sunrise glow,
17   bright message relay they from Sorek,
18   light reflected, light received,
19   the watchtower of my heart hath sent
20   the beard of flame to hugeness.
21   CHORUS: Sorek, you say? Your words escape my belief.
22   CHAD: Delilah lies in Sorek. Is that not clear enough?
23   CHORUS: Delilah lies. No truer words e'er spoken.
24   CHAD: Am I a lad, that you address me so?
25   CHORUS: No lad, a judge, a hero born for greatness.
26   CHAD: Then Sorek shall be mine. Like fabled Neptune,
27   swift-fleeing Argos over Dirce's stream,
28   for his love too, dwelt in a foreign land,
29   close to the rock of Pallas, for once
30   the Lord Poseidon, Ruler of the Sea...
31   CLINT: Wait just a minute. How did Poseidon get into
32   the story?
33   CHAD: Greek Tragedy, remember?
34   JOE: More like *geek* tragedy.

1   BONNI: Joe's right. There's no action in Greek drama.
2   Everything exciting happens off-stage.
3   WENDY: I think we should emulate Shakespeare. After all,
4   he wrote the best plays that have ever been written.
5   CASEY: Really? Is he the one who wrote *Bill and Ted's*
6   *Excellent Adventure?*
7   CLINT: All right, let's pick up the story right where we left
8   off, but this time, make it sound Shakespearean.
9   JOE: Great! For mine own part, that was Greek to me.
10   *(MELISSA climbs on chair to represent a balcony. CASEY*
11   *kneels in front of the chair. All others wait nearby.)*
12   MELISSA: Samson, oh, Samson, wherefore art thou,
13   Samson?
14   CASEY: What light through yonder window breaks? It is
15   the east, and Delilah is the sun.
16   JOE: Entice him to see wherein his great strength lieth.
17   BONNI: Some Cupid kills with arrows, some with traps.
18   CHAD: Discover the means by which we may prevail
19   against him, and bind him to afflict him.
20   MELISSA: *(To others)* If it were done, when it is done, then
21   it were well it were done quickly.
22   BONNI: We will give thee every one of us eleven hundred
23   pieces of silver, for all that glitters is not gold.
24   MELISSA: Very well, but say of me not that I loved Samson
25   less, but that I loved silver more.
26   CASEY: She's beautiful; and therefore to be wooed;
27   She is a woman; and therefore to be won.
28   MELISSA: Tell me wherein thy great strength lieth, and
29   wherewith thou mightiest be bound to afflict thee.
30   CASEY: *(Aside)* By the pricking of my thumbs, something
31   wicked this way comes. *(To DELILAH)* Bind me with
32   seven green vines, then shall I be weak.
33   WENDY: Now is the winter of our discontent
34   Made glorious summer by this revelation.

1 JOE: Nothing in his life becomes him like the leaving it.
2 MELISSA: The Philistines be upon thee, Samson. Screw
3   thy courage to the sticking-place.
4 CASEY: I tricked you, 'tis not in the bond.
5 MELISSA: Thou canst not say I did it; never shake thy gory
6   locks at me.
7 CASEY: *(Aside)* I dare not tell her the truth; that would be
8   the most unkindest cut of all.
9 CLINT: No! Stop! Quit! Cut!
10 MELISSA: That's what I was trying to do.
11 CLINT: This will never work. No one reads Shakespeare
12   anymore. They'll never catch all those obscure
13   references.
14 BONNI: You're right. It's so unfamiliar they might think
15   they are Scripture references.
16 CLINT: We have to write a script that will be understood
17   by today's audience.
18 BONNI: How about melodrama?
19 CLINT: Melodrama?
20 JOE: You know, heroes and villains and maidens in distress.
21 CLINT: Well, I can't quite imagine Delilah as a maiden in
22   distress, but let's give it a try. *(BONNI and JOE sit on
23   two chairs side by side while the others hide behind
24   them. CLINT, as the narrator, stands to one side.)* **There's
25   trouble galore in Sorek Gulch where our hero, Sam
26   Strongman, has been courting the beautiful but
27   fragile Delilah Dimplechaser, daughter of the village
28   barber. We now continue with our story, *The Barber
29   of Sorek or Hair Today, Gone Tomorrow.***
30 BONNI: Oh, Sam, what am I going to do? Phil S. Stine, the
31   evil banker of Sorek Gulch, is going to foreclose the
32   mortgage on my father's barber shop if we don't give
33   him what he wants.
34 JOE: What does he want, this evil banker of Sorek Gulch?

1   **Your father's scissors so he can clip his coupons? He**
2   **should steal from the Squeaky Clean Washateria**
3   **instead so he can launder his money.**
4   **CHAD: I heard that, Strongman. You may have muscles,**
5   **but Phil S. Stine has a brain.**
6   **JOE: Really? Where do you keep it? Over at the bank in a**
7   **brain trust, or down at the jail in a brain cell? You**
8   **obviously don't carry it around with you.**
9   **CHAD: This is you final warning, Delilah Dimplechaser.**
10   **Either you give me what I want, or your father will be**
11   **cut from his job and sent to the minors. That would**
12   **be "shear" disaster.**
13   **BONNI: Oh, no, not the miners. He's not strong enough to**
14   **dig.**
15   **CHAD: Then you'll have to find a substitute. Someone who**
16   **is strong enough. Do you dig it, Sam?** *(CHAD exits to*
17   *behind the chairs.)*
18   **BONNI: Oh, Sam, you're so strong. How did you get all**
19   **those muscles?**
20   **JOE: Well, I saw this ad in the back of a magazine about a**
21   **fellow named Charles Atlas, and...**
22   **BONNI: Oh, Sam. You're mocking me. Don't you love me?**
23   **JOE: Oh, Delilah, of course I adore you. Didn't I bring you**
24   **those gates from the city of Gaza?**
25   **BONNI: Then tell me how you got to be so strong.**
26   **JOE: Well, it really wasn't too difficult. I haven't had a bath**
27   **in over a month.**
28   **BONNI: Oh, Sam, how can you tease me like that? If you**
29   **don't tell me the secret of your strength, I will have to**
30   **marry Phil S. Stine and become Delilah Stine, and**
31   **then if I have a son, he would be Frank N. Stine.**
32   **JOE: The secret of my strength...** *(Others peek around all*
33   *sides of the chairs.)*
34   **ALL: Yes?**

1 **JOE: Delilah, are we alone?**
2 **BONNI: Of course. Why do you ask?**
3 **JOE: I had the distinct feeling just then that we had an**
4   **audience.**
5 **CHAD:** *(Standing up behind the chair)* **Whew, that was a**
6   **close shave.**
7 **JOE: The secret of my strength lies in my long hair.**
8 **BONNI: Really?**
9 **JOE: Yes. My long hair and my great mind make me a**
10   **hairy reasoner.**
11 **BONNI:** *(Weeping)* **Ohhh! You don't love me. You want me**
12   **to marry Phil.**
13 **JOE: All right! All right! Take my hair and weave it into the**
14   **rug your mother is making on that loom.**
15 **BONNI: Then you will be weak?**
16 **JOE: Sure. People will be able to walk all over me.**
17 **ALL: Boo! Hiss!**
18 **CLINT: Hey, you're not supposed to boo the hero.**
19 **COLLEEN: We're not booing him, it's just that terrible**
20   **joke.**
21 **CLINT: This whole approach is terrible. What we need is**
22   **something that will be familiar to a church audience.**
23   **Most of them have probably never seen Greek**
24   **Tragedy or Shakespeare or melodrama.**
25 **COLLEEN: You're right. There's only one type of drama all**
26   **of them have seen.**
27 **CASEY: Wayne's World?**
28 **MELISSA: Not!**
29 **COLLEEN: They are all familiar with the most famous**
30   **religious dramatic art of all – the Sunday school**
31   **Christmas pageant.**
32 **CLINT: Of course. Why didn't I think of that from the**
33   **start? We need to do this story in the style of a Sunday**
34   **school pageant. Take your places, everyone.** *(All form*

1   *a straight line. The middle six have large letters forming*
2   *the word S-A-M-S-O-N.)*
3   **COLLEEN: From far and near we gather**
4   **On this exciting night.**
5   **We've worked so hard to learn our lines**
6   **I hope we say them right.**
7   **We all are in position,**
8   **We want to welcome you,**
9   **We've worked so hard to learn our lines (oops)**
10   **Because it's really true.**
11   **CHAD: "S" is for strength**
12   **Because Samson was strong.**
13   **MELISSA: "A" is for all of**
14   **The things he did wrong.**
15   **JOE: "M" is for men**
16   **Who were lying in wait.**
17   **WENDY: "S" is for scissors**
18   **That sealed Samson's fate.**
19   **CASEY: "O" is for "Open**
20   **Your eyes from their sleep."**
21   **BONNI: "N" is for Nazarite,**
22   **The vow he didn't keep.**
23   **CLINT: Now we've spelled Samson.**
24   **The story you know.**
25   **Our part is all finished.**
26   **We're going to go.**
27   *(All move out of line.)*
28   **CLINT:** *(Continued)* **Well? What do you think?**
29   **CHAD: It will certainly be familiar to church audiences.**
30   **CLINT: Exactly.**
31   **BONNI: And it does tell the story of Samson.**
32   **CLINT: Right! It's just exactly what we need. Let's meet**
33   **Saturday morning at nine o'clock for practice, and**
34   **afterward I'll see that everyone gets a bag of candy.**

CHAPTER FOUR

A Fight in the Church

Developing Conflict

Imagine the following story: The first day Esther arrived in the court of King Ahasuerus, she met a man named Haman. She introduced him to her cousin, Mordecai, and the three of them became good friends. The end.

Why is that story basically uninteresting while the story of Esther recorded in the Bible has retained its fascination for thousands of years? The answer is conflict. In the biblical story of Esther, Haman hates Mordecai, and because of that hatred decides to destroy an entire race of people. Will he achieve his goal or will Esther and Mordecai be able to stop him? The suspense is heightened by the revelation that the new Queen is a Jewess. The hatred of Haman grows stronger during that great scene of irony where he is compelled to lead Mordecai through the city on the King's horse yelling, "Thus shall it be done unto the man whom the King delighteth to honor" (Esther 6:9). The conflict grows as the announced date for the destruction of the Jews draws nearer and it boils over as Haman attends the Queen's banquets, learns of her nationality and, falling before her to plead for his life, is assumed by the King to be forcing her in the very palace. The resolution comes swiftly — Haman is hanged on the gallows he had made for Mordecai.

Conflict results when two opposing forces clash, resulting in action. That pattern of conflict and resolution is the basic element for the construction of a sketch. People will gather to see a fight, whether on the playground or in a great sports arena. To retain the interest of the audience in a sketch, you must give them conflict.

"Girl asks boy to tell her his secret. He does." That is the way it often happens in life, but it's really not very interesting. "Girl asks boy to tell her his secret so she can reveal it to his enemies.

He teases her four times before finally telling the truth." Now we have the conflict between Samson and Delilah.

"Man and woman get married and have a child." Again, a common occurrence but hardly the stuff for drama. "Man and woman get married and can't have children. Wife talks husband into having a child with a surrogate, then grows jealous of the child who was born because they finally have a child of their own." Now you have conflict and the story of Abraham and Sarah.

Five Types of Conflict

Drama theorists have identified five types of conflict which are commonly used in the construction of scripts. All of these are evident in the stories which God chose to record for us in the Bible.

1. Man Against Man

Even when other types of conflict exist in a story, the conflict between two people is usually present. It may involve actual battle, like the one which took place between David and Goliath. It may involve the refusal to fight, as in the story of David and Saul where David proved he was the right man to rule Israel by refusing to wrest control from a God-appointed king. The conflict may involve nations and cosmic events, as in the story of Moses freeing his people from the iron furnace of Egypt. Although magicians, priests and millions of common people and soldiers get involved, the basic conflict comes between Moses and the Pharaoh.

2. Main Against Nature

It might be argued that this type of conflict, when it relates to Bible characters, should better be understood as a conflict between man and God. It is true that God is in control of nature, but if that argument were carried to the extreme, it could be shown that God is in control of everything. Therefore, all conflict would be seen as man against God. Even though insurance companies like to describe great natural catastrophes as "acts of

God," the truth is that for the most part, God allows nature to act according to its own laws.

What needs to be recognized here is that there were Bible characters who fought against nature, whether they saw the hand of God in it or not. When Elijah faced the great wind, and the earthquake and the fire on Mount Horeb (I Kings 19:11), he was trying to survive the destructive force of nature, even though he knew theologically that God had allowed those forces to confront him. When Jonah spent his time in the fish's belly, he was in conflict with a natural catastrophe. Conflict with nature entered into the story of Moses and Pharaoh, with much of the increase in tension arising from the fact that Pharaoh refused to believe the God of Moses was actually controlling the plagues.

Because the environment permeates the news to such a degree in this age, a sketch writer should take a particularly close look at this area of conflict. Try applying the situation in Ephesians 2:14 to environmentalists and lumbermen within a church instead of Jews and Gentiles.

3. Man Against Society.

Some of the most memorable characters in literature are those men and women who refused to conform to the society around them, even though it cost them dearly to take such a stand. Traditions, customs, fads and fashions all call for a conformity which only a very strong-willed person can oppose.

The Old Testament prophets stand out as those who opposed the corrupt society in which they lived in order to call that society back to a proper worship of Jehovah. Isaiah opposed the national policy of an alliance with Babylon. He described in detail the fashions of the day, which revealed the haughtiness of the people: "The rings and nose jewels, the changeable suits of apparel, and the mantles, and the wimples, and the crisping pins" (Isa. 3:21-22). Jeremiah was accused of treason because he predicted the fall of Jerusalem and weakened the will of the people to fight and defend the city. Later he encouraged the remnant to stay in the land, but they rejected his advice and left for Egypt, taking him along with them by force.

41

Ezekiel opposed the false worship of the nation during the period of the Babylonian captivity, singling out for special scorn those who brought their worship of "creeping things and abominable beasts" (Eze. 8:10) into "the chambers of his imagery" (vs. 12).

But there are other examples of those who came into conflict with society as well. Rahab risked the wrath of the city of Jericho when she hid the two spies from Joshua. Daniel and his companions stood firm in the face of pressure from the entire political and religious structure of Babylon. Christ taught many truths which brought him into conflict with the religious society of his day. Eventually, those religious leaders were able to turn the political structure against him as well.

Contemporary situations where a Christian might come into conflict with society include the abortion question, political correctness, homelessness, corruption in politics, violence and immorality in the broadcast media, drug messages and sexual innuendos in rock music.

4. Man Against Himself

A person comes in conflict with himself when two aspects of his personality clash. This requires the writer to develop characters who are more than one-dimensional. A hero has to reveal some weakness in order to come into conflict with himself, but it is this very revelation of weakness which will make that character more believable to an audience. The apostle Paul knew this inner conflict and wrote many times about the struggle between his new nature, which wanted to honor God, and his old nature, which still delighted in evil. "For what I do is not the good I want to do; no, the evil I do not want to do — this I keep on doing" (Rom. 7:19 NIV).

Samson provides an example of a man in conflict with himself throughout his entire life. On the one hand, he lived under a life-long religious vow and served as a judge over his people. On the other hand, he found himself involved repeatedly in illicit liaisons with the women of his enemies, the Philistines. The frustration of living that way eventually destroyed him.

Christians come into conflict with self constantly as a result of progressive sanctification. Paul called it a conflict between the "old man" and the "new man" who do battle for control of the believer (Rom. 6:6). A playwright can use this conflict to persuasive advantage by employing a technique called *cognitive dissonance.* Through drama, people can be shown that what they are doing does not agree with what they say they believe. Topics which fit well into this area of conflict include love, peace, long-suffering, kindness, gossip, faithfulness, compassion, charity and encouragement.

5. Man Against Fate

This type of conflict, even more than that of man against nature, is subject to theological debate. Fate is usually considered to be some mysterious force which determines the destiny of an individual and which cannot be changed. When you introduce a personal God into an individual's life, then fate no longer exists. Yet there are those who, even with a personal God, would argue that man's destiny is predetermined and unchanging. Others would say that God has given humans a free will and the ability to change their destinies.

Whatever view a person chooses to take, tremendous dramatic conflict exists between people and those elements of life they are not able to control. The man born blind who appealed to Christ for healing realized that he did not have the ability to change his condition. Joseph did not choose his family, did not choose to be sold into Egypt and did not choose to be purchased as a slave by Potiphar. Yet each of those "fates" brought him into great conflict. The attitude which Joseph eventually adopted toward these uncontrollable circumstances of life was that "God meant it unto good" (Gen. 50:20), but he didn't always see it that way.

If you identify "fate" with the hand of God, then even more examples of conflict come to mind. Jonah flees from God, only to discover that there is no hiding place from the Almighty. Nebuchadnezzar opposes God and spends seven years in exile, feeding on grass like an ox until he recognizes the sovereignty of

God. Zedekiah disputes Jeremiah's prophecy from God that Jerusalem will fall to the Babylonians. When he is captured, they kill his sons before him and then put out his eyes so the death of his boys will be the last thing he remembers. Wicked King Ahab and his notorious Queen Jezebel introduce Baal worship into Israel in opposition to God. Ahab dies in battle, and Jezebel is thrown from a window and trampled by horses.

Another method of developing conflict in your plays is to think of it in terms of suspense. It is important to introduce your main character to some conflict near the beginning of the sketch which will cause the audience to develop a strong interest in seeing how that conflict will be resolved. This may involve danger, disaster, a threat or an expectation of something good. If the audience likes a character, there is an immediate suspense created concerning how events will turn out for that person they like. In comedies particularly, the suspense is created simply by an interest in what will happen next to this person they like.

Various methods may be used to increase the suspense in a drama. If the main character is in danger, a new danger can be introduced each time the present danger is resolved. The growth in suspense will be greatest if it is the solving of one problem which actually creates the new danger. In order to maintain suspense throughout the entire drama, the main objective of the protagonist should not be achieved until the climax. The overcoming of each danger then becomes one step in the conquest of the great prize.

Many obstacles can be introduced to keep a hero from the goal. In the story of David and Goliath, the great conflict David faces is the battle with the giant. But before he can win that battle, he must overcome the objections of his brothers and the skepticism of the King. He has to try on and reject wearing the armor he is offered, a decision which increases his danger. He has to make the choice to face heavy armor with a slingshot. He has to cross the valley enduring the taunts of the Philistine hero. The introduction of each of these elements increases the suspense because we realize that each decision David makes is true to his character.

Another method of building suspense is to have one character make a decision which affects the lives of others. This is the basic method of suspense in the development of a courtroom drama. The question in the mind of the audience throughout the play concerns the verdict the judge or jury will render. It is an essential element in the story of Esther, who faced the choice of risking her own life by approaching the king without an invitation in order to possibly save the lives of her entire race. Mordecai appealed to her on that basis by telling her that she might well have come to be queen "for such a time as this" (Esther 4:14).

In my play *Prince of Peace* which deals with the events of the Apocalypse, the villain offers to rescind an execution order if the protagonist chooses to deny her Messiah. Suspense and conflict increase as the decision is faced.

DAVID: I propose a test. We shall call is a test of faith. That has a good ring to it, wouldn't you say? Yacov shall be first. My soldiers will take him outside and prepare their weapons. Then the test will begin with Sharona. It is a very simple test, my dear. You will be given a choice. Your husband – or your Messiah.

YACOV: No! You beast!

DAVID: I believe that is what your Jesus called me. I wouldn't want to make him a liar now, would I? Men, take this gentleman out to the firing squad and wait for my command. We are about to conduct a test – a test of faith.

SHARONA: Yacov, I can't.

YACOV: You must. "My beloved is mine and I am his. Until the daybreak and the shadows flee away. Until the daybreak..." (Song 2:16-17) *(SOLDIERS exit with YACOV.)*

RAHEL: "The Lord is my keeper..." (Ps. 121:5)

DAVID: Are you ready for your test, Mrs. Shimon? I have the power to save your husband and I have the power to kill. What power does your Messiah have? "Ask and it shall be given"?

RAHEL: "The Lord is thy shade upon thy right hand." (Ps. 121:5)

DAVID: Just say the word, and Yacov will go free. The choice is yours, Sharona.

RAHEL: "He shall preserve thy soul." (Ps. 121:7) *(ILYA slaps RAHEL.)*

ILYA: Your turn will come, old woman. You shall choose for the life of your daughter. Then we shall see if your precious words give you strength.

DAVID: Come, Mrs. Shimon. What will it be? Others are anxious to take their test as well.

SHARONA: I cannot...I cannot deny my Lord. *(DAVID steps to the door.)*

DAVID: Fire!

SFX: Two shots.

Obstacles, then, can occur through events or through antagonists. The stronger the antagonist you introduce into your play, the greater will be the danger for your hero or heroine. If both the protagonist and the antagonist want the same thing, the conflict will grow as each one seeks to achieve the desired goal and keep the other from having it. The strength of your conflict depends on the strength of the main character, the intensity with which he seeks his goal and the strength of the opposition. If those three elements are chosen well, conflict will be the inevitable result.

A very simple conflict resulting from mistaken identity forms the basis for the sketch *Patsy* which appears at the end of Chapter Six. Derived from an actual incident in the life of Mrs. George Washington, it illustrates how a historical play can teach scriptural truth.

The following sketch, *Guided Tour,* introduces a message or series of sermons on the book of Philippi. Notice how even in a two-person scene the conflict develops character and establishes the relationship between the protagonist and the antagonist.

Guided Tour

by Robert A. Allen

"But isn't it true that the only extant writing we have
today concerning the city of Philippi is a
religious writing — from the Bible?"

CAST OF CHARACTERS

Guide

Employed by the government of Greece, he prides himself
on his knowledge of ancient history. He has worked as a guide
for thirty years and has given his speeches so many times that
they have become almost mechanical.

Tourist

On his first tour of Bible lands, the Tourist has a genuine
desire to learn all that he can about the historical sites they are
visiting. He is more concerned about biblical accuracy than
historical conjecture.

PRODUCTION NOTES

The GUIDE dresses casually and carries a walking stick which he uses often to punctuate his remarks.

The TOURIST wears comfortable walking clothes and has two cameras slung about his neck.

The scene is the excavations in the city of Philippi, Greece. The time is the present.

1   **GUIDE: Welcome to Philippi! This ancient city, the ruins**
2   **of which lie before you today, was built by the**
3   **famous King Philip of Macedon, the father of**
4   **Alexander the Great. As you know, we have come**
5   **just eight miles from the Aegean coast in this**
6   **country known today as Greece. As an important**
7   **gold mining center, the city was very rich. But Philip**
8   **chose to build here not because of the gold, but**
9   **because of the strategic location. Philippi controls**
10   **the major pass through the mountains which sepa-**
11   **rate Europe from Asia. By fortifying Philippi, he**
12   **controlled the best route from east to west. During**
13   **Roman days, Mark Antony and Octavian defeated**
14   **two of Julius Caesar's assassins, Brutus and Cassius**
15   **at Philipi. It is these great historic events which**
16   **make our visit to Philippi so interesting.**
17   **TOURIST: Sir, if I might – a question?**
18   **GUIDE: Certainly. What is it?**
19   **TOURIST: Well, sir. Did Paul ever stop here?**
20   **GUIDE: Sure! Sure! Paul! Paul! But who is Paul when**
21   **compared to Augustus and Antony and Octavian?**
22   **TOURIST: The apostle Paul. Didn't he preach here?**
23   **GUIDE:** *(Shrugging the question aside)* **Possibly. But cities**
24   **aren't remembered because of preachers. Cities are**
25   **remembered because of emperors and conquerors**
26   **and politicians who visited them. Augustus the**
27   **emperor founded a military colony in this place – the**
28   **"Colonia Augusta Julia Philippensis." Philippi was a**
29   **miniature likeness of the greatest city in all the**
30   **world, Rome itself.**
31   **TOURIST:** *(Raising his hand)* **Sir, if I might?**
32   **GUIDE: Now what?**
33   **TOURIST: Did anyone ever write a history of Philippi, sir?**
34   **GUIDE: Of course not. The people who lived here weren't**

1   important – only the ones who came here to visit.
2   Philip and Mark Antony and Octavian...
3   TOURIST: And Paul?
4   GUIDE: Listen, fellow. I don't know what kind of religious
5   fanatic you are, but I don't appreciate you always
6   trying to bring religion into history.
7   TOURIST: But isn't it true that the only extant writing
8   we have today concerning the city of Philippi is a
9   religious writing – from the Bible?
10   GUIDE: I suppose you could put it that way.
11   TOURIST: Written by the apostle Paul?
12   GUIDE: Some people seem to think so.
13   TOURIST: Written about a church which Paul started on a
14   visit to the city?
15   GUIDE: Yes, if you choose to believe the Bible. We don't
16   have any other record of Paul's supposed visit.
17   TOURIST: That's interesting. Another question, if I might.
18   GUIDE: Go ahead. You've ruined the lecture already.
19   TOURIST: Are there manuscripts in existence which tell
20   about Philip and Octavian visiting here? Any letters
21   they wrote to people at the military base?
22   GUIDE: Of course not.
23   TOURIST: Then couldn't we say that most of what we
24   really know about Philippi in ancient times we know
25   because of Paul's letter to the church there?
26   GUIDE: Preposterous! Now, if you will come this way, we
27   will look at the ruins of the military colony.
28   TOURIST: And the prison?
29   GUIDE: Have you been here before? How did you know
30   about the prison?
31   TOURIST: Well, Luke wrote about how Paul was put in
32   prison along with Silas, so I figured there had to be
33   one somewhere in the city.
34   GUIDE: Paul, again!

1   TOURIST: While Paul and Silas were in prison, they
2   decided to have a singspiration. But they didn't have
3   any accompaniment, so God sent an earthquake – to
4   provide them with a rhythm section, I guess. The next
5   day the magistrates found out they were Roman citi-
6   zens, and they came over in person to beg the
7   prisoners' forgiveness.
8   GUIDE: What did you call them?
9   TOURIST: Paul and Silas.
10   GUIDE: No, the officers.
11   TOURIST: Magistrates?
12   GUIDE: And you said that Roman magistrates imprisoned
13   Roman citizens?
14   TOURIST: Yes, if you believe the Bible.
15   GUIDE: Imprisoning a citizen was the serious charge
16   brought by Cicero against Verres. To falsely accuse a
17   Roman citizen was punishable by death. The Bible
18   says they begged forgiveness of prisoners? Tell me
19   more about his Book of Philippi.
20   TOURIST: Well, there was no Jewish synagogue in the city.
21   GUIDE: That's right. There seems to have been only a very
22   small Jewish population – not even the ten men
23   necessary for a synagogue. Instead they met...
24   TOURIST: Down by the riverside.
25   GUIDE: That's right, but...
26   TOURIST: That's where Paul met Lydia, a purple-dye
27   merchant from Thyatira who was a proselyte to
28   Judaism. When Lydia heard Paul and Silas preach
29   about Jesus, she accepted him as her Savior. She was
30   the very first person in all of Europe who became a
31   Christian.
32   GUIDE: Here in Philippi? European Christianity began
33   right here?
34   TOURIST: Right here.

1   **GUIDE:** *(Recovering himself and trying to get on with his*
2   *planned lecture)* **Well, that is all very interesting. But**
3   **I really think we'd better get on with our tour. Now**
4   **over here we have the marketplace, a typical eastern**
5   **marketplace where people would bring their wares**
6   **to sell.**
7   **TOURIST: The marketplace? How exciting. That's why**
8   **Paul and Silas were in jail, you know. There was this**
9   **fortuneteller...**
10   **GUIDE:** *(Ignoring him, addresses the rest of the tourists.)* **The**
11   **people would sit in little booths along the sides of the**
12   **streets and offer to sell food or carpets, or maybe to**
13   **tell someone's fortune.**
14   **TOURIST: She made lots of money for her masters until**
15   **Paul and Silas came along.**
16   **GUIDE:** *(Still ignoring him)* **Every day the marketplace**
17   **would fill up with people. It was the center of social**
18   **life in the city. There was always a lot of money**
19   **changing hands.**
20   **TOURIST:** *(Continues on as if the GUIDE is substantiating*
21   *everything he is saying.)* **When she saw them, she would**
22   **run down the street, following them and yelling,**
23   **"These men are the servants of the Most High God**
24   **which show unto us the way of salvation."** (Dan. 3:26)
25   **GUIDE: There were always disturbances in the market-**
26   **place. Fights were quite common. So right in the**
27   **center of the market, a large chair was placed for the**
28   **magistrate.**
29   **TOURIST: She did this many days. Then one day Paul tired**
30   **of it, so he turned around and commanded the spirit**
31   **of divination to come out of her, and it did.**
32   **GUIDE: If there was any problem between buyers and**
33   **sellers, they could come to the magistrate to get it**
34   **settled. Of course, there was always the expectation**

1   **that they would bring along a gift to make it worth**
2   **the magistrate's time.**
3   **TOURIST: That really made the girl's masters angry. Now**
4   **she couldn't tell fortunes anymore, and they couldn't**
5   **make any money. So they grabbed Paul and Silas and**
6   **dragged them in front of the magistrate.**
7   **GUIDE:** *(Still ignoring TOURIST)* **It wasn't a very efficient**
8   **way to administer judgment. Everyone shouted out**
9   **his case and all the while, numerous bribes were**
10   **changing hands.**
11   **TOURIST:** *(Nodding agreement)* **That's how they ended up**
12   **in prison. The magistrates listened to the masters of**
13   **the girl and had Paul and Silas beaten and thrown**
14   **into prison.**
15   **GUIDE:** *(Having finished his prepared speech)* **Well, I think**
16   **it's time to get back on the bus and head off to the next**
17   **town. You'll love it. Why, Caesar Augustus actually**
18   **slept there.**
19   **TOURIST: What about Paul? Did he visit there?**
20   **GUIDE:** *(Exasperated)* **How should I know?**
21   **TOURIST: Well, if not, I think I'll just stay here in Philippi.**
22   **GUIDE: Suit yourself. All right, everybody *else*. Back on**
23   **the bus.**
24
25
26
27
28
29
30
31
32
33
34

CHAPTER FIVE

Did Daniel Really Worry About Skin Blemishes?

Developing Characters

The biblical account of the instructions given by King Nebuchadnezzar to those who are bringing him the best of the captives from the city of Jerusalem includes the command that they were to be "children in whom was no blemish" (Dan. 1:4). Although this meant much more than the facial blemishes which plague today's teenager, it serves to remind us that Daniel and his friends were real people. They actually lived and they faced the minor frustrations and skin problems which bother teens today at the same time that they were facing the climactic political problems which gained them a place in the biblical record.

There is a tendency when dramatizing the lives of biblical characters to portray them without their blemishes. It is almost as if we're afraid it would be sacrilegious to suggest that these people had real problems. But the result of such an approach is to render them lifeless and unbelievable. One of the greatest advantages of using drama in the church is the opportunity to present biblical characters in such a way as to make audiences realize that they lived lives very similar to our own. Once they realize that, they will be able to identify with these people and profit from the manner in which they learned to trust God in the midst of their problems. If they come across as supermen or superwomen, their experiences will not be of practical help to today's believer.

Once you have a theme and a conflict, you are ready to start developing characters. In adaptation, which is what you are doing if you use a Bible story as your idea, your characters will already be somewhat familiar. But you would be wise to follow the same process as if you were creating totally new characters. This process includes describing the characters, naming them, deciding how they fit into the plot and placing them into action.

What Makes a Character?

There are certain characteristics which are true of almost all cast members in dramas. They are usually more articulate than people in real life. Listen to the conversations taking place in a crowded room and ask yourself how many people you hear who are speaking clearly and concisely without undue hesitation. How much of the conversation is truly witty and intelligent? Unless you have dropped into the middle of an unusual group, you will probably find yourself quickly bored. Well-developed stage characters are never boring. Even when a character is a bore on stage, he is an *interesting* bore. A writer must develop characters who can keep talking because a sketch is expected to have a continual flow of dialog.

Stage characters are also less complex than real-life personalities. An audience cannot spend several years learning to know and love your characters. They must form their opinions in the first few minutes of the sketch. This doesn't mean that characters should be cartoon-like or one-dimensional, but it does mean that their personality traits should be obvious through their words, actions and expressions.

The personality traits of stage characters are also exaggerated. You may know people who are jealous, but the jealousy of the characters in your sketch must be greater than that of your acquaintances. It must be a jealousy which drives them to action. So you exaggerate the jealousy. You may know people who are proud or foolish or stupid, but to make interesting stage characters, they must be prouder or more foolish or more stupid than the people most of us know. Very few people ever have the opportunity to be heroes in everyday existence, but a sketch almost always demands a hero. An audience attends a dramatic performance in order to witness events and see characters who are larger than life.

Which brings us back to Daniel. On the one hand, we want the audience to identify with him, to know that he is a real person. On the other hand, we want them to see in him certain characteristics which are greater than the average person possesses, traits which make him a hero whose story is worthy of the audience's time. In a way it is a dilemma, but resolving that dilemma produces truly memorable characters. In any historical sketch where research forms the basis for character development, imagination is still essential in order to make your subjects live for your audience.

The description of your characters does not belong in the cast list. The cast of characters, on the first page of the sketch, should contain a list of names, a statement concerning occupation, age, and any mannerisms which are necessary for character development. Biographical details beyond that will be read only by the director and will be used by him only if he happens to have actors available which fit your description. Otherwise they will be ignored.

The place to describe your characters is within the script itself. Costumes will aid in identification to some degree. A king in rich robes and a crown will be recognized immediately as someone important. However, Bible-based sketches costumed in modern dress usually help make the story seem more contemporary to an audience. In that case, you would need to suggest a modern costume which would arouse the same sense of worth as the rich robe — clothes with designer labels, for example, or warm-up jackets with professional ball team logos. Costumes can reveal character by being fashionable or unfashionable, gaudy or cheap, filthy or well-kept, colorful or somber.

In addition to costumes, the appearance of actors should suggest to the audience their character traits. Does this person look healthy or frail? Does he have a relaxed expression which suggests a calm spirit? Does she look wrinkled or lined or pale, conveying a spirit of bitterness or less of resolution? Some of these details will be up to the actors and director, but they should be suggested by the writer by means of a few choice descriptive words the first time a character appears.

A person's speech will reveal much concerning personality. Vocabulary indicates education and native intelligence as well as cultural background. What she talks about lets us know her interests, her background, her goals and her peeves. Be certain that your characters do not all sound alike. Each individual should be able to tell the same story and give it a different twist which reveals his point of view. A good exercise in character development would be to try just that with the people in your sketch. Write out the identical incident the way each of them would report it and listen to the words they choose.

How a person speaks also tells much about herself. Does she speak with a rapid-fire delivery, or slowly, with hesitations, thinking carefully before saying anything? Does he enter boldly into conversations with great self-confidence, or is his speech timid and weak? Does she use long sentences or short, precise answers?

Actions present one of the best methods the writer has for revealing character. These may include mannerisms such as coughing repeatedly, polishing fingernails, cracking knuckles or pacing. A woman who picks up imaginary pieces of lint and dusts furniture with her finger tells the audience she is concerned with appearance, maybe even a perfectionist. In those actions they might recognize a Martha from Luke 10 even before anyone calls her by name. The way a man handles money could show the difference between the greedy Judas and the generous Good Samaritan.

The great motivational sequences of the sketch will also demonstrate character. The action of the plot should be designed in such a way that the audience not only sees what people are doing but also understands why they are doing those things. A person who throws rocks at someone because they are of a different nationality would be considered a bully and a racist. But a David who throws rocks at a Goliath is considered a hero, because he is motivated by a desire to rescue his country from domination by a vicious enemy.

Stage Actions

Stage actions are often divided into two categories: dramatic action and technical action. Technical action is usually left up to the director and involves forming the actors on-stage into visually pleasing groups, arranging for movement such as exits and entrances and focusing the attention of the audience on a particular speaker and part of the stage. Dramatic action, however, should be planned by the writer. These actions create atmosphere, reveal character and advance the plot line.

The opening of your sketch is vital in the creation of the mood or atmosphere of the production. Always start your sketch in the middle of an action sequence which lets the audience know something about the main conflict, the time period and the mood. A sketch about Rahab and the spies could begin with Rahab locking all of her windows, suggesting a danger from outside and foreshadowing the open window through which she would hang the signal of safety when Israel attacked. You might be tempted to have your actors sit and talk for several pages in order to give an audience the background you think is necessary, but you will have a much stronger opening if you show your characters in action.

Everything people do on-stage should reveal something about their character. If a person enters a room without knocking, it shows that she belongs in the house, either because she is part of the household or a welcome guest. If a person sneaks into a room without knocking, it shows he feels guilty about entering without permission. A man who checks his hair in a mirror shows he is vain. A child who throws toys shows anger much more effectively than one who walks in and announces, "I'm mad." Be sure you give people specific actions which tell an audience what they are like.

The actions of your characters should also advance the plot. When King Zedekiah surrenders to the Babylonians, he should take his crown from his head and give it over to them. When Moses enters the court of Pharaoh, he should refuse to bow like all the others are doing. It wasn't Daniel's silent prayers to God which roused the hatred of the other princes, it was his action of opening his window toward Jerusalem and praying publicly three times a day. Don't make your audience guess why a person loves or hates someone else — show them.

Knowing Me, Knowing You

What other people say about a person will also reveal his character. Their words may be motivated by jealousy or pride or hatred, but the audience members who recognize those motivations will form their own opinions of the person under discussion, rather than taking a description at face value. We are already used to doing that in our interpersonal relationships. In order to have your actors reveal the character of others in the most effective manner, remember that actions speak louder than words. Avoid giving long descriptions of how a person looks — instead, write dialog which tells what people have done. "By their fruits ye shall know them" (Matt. 7:20), Jesus told his disciples when warning them about false teachers.

The name you choose for your character can provide some clues to his or her personality. For a comedy you might want to be obvious, using descriptive names such as Will B. Good and Polly Paradise. But for the most part, you will want names to carry a connotation of the person's character without such obvious cuteness. Names do have meanings, and you should name your characters as carefully as you would name your children. Trisha and Emily suggest entirely different personalities than Edna and Florence. Don't be hesitant to change a name during the revision process if it no longer fits the personality which has developed during the writing of the sketch.

People are also known by their friends. Usually a sketch has two main characters: a protagonist and an antagonist. In addition to these, there are secondary or supporting roles, and these characters are friends with either the heroine or the villain. Does your lead remain loyal to friends who misunderstand him? Does your villain demand that his companions obey him whether he is right or wrong? The answers to these and similar questions reveal much about those individuals.

Once you have a good idea of what your characters are like, they will begin to fit into your story. You will have a strong character who has set her mind to achieve a particular goal. She will be your heroine or protagonist. Then you will have someone who is either seeking the same goal or opposing the one who is striving to reach it. She will be your villain or antagonist. Remember, of course, that the conflict could be against nature or society or fate as well as against an individual. It is through these main characters that your audience will follow the story. They should become emotionally involved with them and really care about what happens to them. Everything in the sketch — from the very beginning to the end — should affect them and change their situation. It is best to have them enter soon, be discovered on-stage at the beginning of the sketch or at least be talked about from the start. Once they enter, they must dominate the action, have the most interesting lines and be on-stage the bulk of the time.

Secondary characters are of importance as they relate to and interact with your leads. The audience should not become greatly involved with their stories or emotions. Instead, everything they do should advance the action of the sketch as it reveals the conflict and resolution between your protagonist and antagonist.

Be careful about writing too many characters into the script. There may be good reasons for your decision, such as wanting to create a part for everyone in a particular Sunday school class, but a sketch will be much stronger if you limit the number of characters. The shorter playing time of a sketch works best without the added complication of an unwieldy cast. Many successful scripts have been written for three actors, although it works best when all three are of basically equal importance. On the other hand, plays with large casts are seldom performed either by amateurs or professionals. Versions of the Passion play or Christmas productions with a cast of hundreds may be very impressive to watch, but if you set out to write or produce such a program, you must recognize that the expense of costumes and sets alone will be far beyond the budget of the average church drama troupe. This is one reason why so many churches are turning to sketches in their worship services. Besides being effective, they're easy to produce.

Most plays are written for a cast somewhere between five and twelve. The shorter the sketch, the smaller you should keep the cast. Fifteen people in a three-act might work, but fifteen people in a five-minute sketch would seldom be justified. A drama troupe of eight people could meet regularly and prepare sketches involving three or four members of the troupe at a time. This would not place a great demand on any of them.

The following sketch first appeared in *Young World* and is reprinted by permission from the Saturday Evening Post Company. The small cast makes it ideal for presentation in a church setting. Applicable sermon topics include hypocrisy, pride and false appearances as described in 1 Samuel 16:7.

Patsy

by Robert A. Allen

"Mr. Washington calls me Patsy.
I've been with the family a long time."

CAST OF CHARACTERS

Pasty

A plainly dressed middle-aged woman. She has been doing some cleaning and appears to be the family maid.

Clarinda Vanderhoofen

A fifty-year-old lady who prides herself on setting the tone for society in New York.

Eustace Dinwiddie

The best friend and sincere admirer of Mrs. Vanderhoofen.

Eleanor Custis

A girl of twelve.

PRODUCTION NOTES

The scene is the front hallway of the Samuel Osgood home in New York which served as the first executive mansion. The year is 1789. The characters should dress to reflect the times.

1 *AT RISE:* PATSY greets CLARINDA and EUSTACE at the door.

2

3 PATSY: Please be seated, ladies. I'm afraid you've caught

4   us quite unprepared. We weren't expecting anyone

5   for the afternoon reception until three o'clock.

6 CLARINDA: That's quite all right. We always try to arrive

7   early, don't we, Eustace dear? We expected you to be

8   unprepared, didn't we, Eustace?

9 EUSTACE: Oh, yes, Mrs. Vanderhoofen, yes, indeed. No one

10   is ever prepared for our arrival, it seems.

11 CLARINDA: Well, we may as well remain, as long as we're

12   here. You may announce our arrival to the president

13   and his wife. I'm sure they'll want some time with us

14   before the reception begins. Reception crowds are so

15   boring, aren't they, Eustace dear?

16 EUSTACE: Oh, yes, Mrs. Vanderhoofen. Very boring, I'm

17   sure. Everything you say, Clarinda.

18 PATSY: I'll be glad to tell Mr. Washington you've arrived.

19   That is, I will when he arrives. He hasn't returned yet

20   from meeting with the Continental Congress. We're

21   expecting him any time now.

22 CLARINDA: I'm sure he's a busy man, but certainly Mrs.

23   Washington could visit with us. She doesn't have

24   anything else scheduled for today, I'm sure. By the

25   way, what is your name, dear?

26 PATSY: Mr. Washington calls me Patsy. I've been with the

27   family a long time. We are very busy getting ready for

28   the reception. Was there something special you

29   wished to discuss?

30 CLARINDA: Well, I must say you are quite forward for a

31   maid. I'm certain it is none of your business what we

32   wish to discuss with Mrs. Washington. Don't you

33   agree, Eustace dear?

34 EUSTACE: Oh, yes, Clarinda. None of her business, I'm sure.

1   **PATSY:** *(Obviously amused about something)* **Well, fine. If**
2   **you don't wish to tell me...but I'm sure Mrs.**
3   **Washington will want to know. She prefers not to be**
4   **disturbed before her receptions unless it is very**
5   **important.**
6   **CLARINDA:** *(To EUSTACE)* **They were right, Eustace dear.**
7   **She's a real snob. "Prefers not to be disturbed!" I'm**
8   **not sure we want her in our circle.**
9   **EUSTACE:** *(To CLARINDA)* **You're right, I'm sure, Clarinda.**
10   **She wouldn't fit in our circle.**
11   **CLARINDA: But she *is* the president's wife, Eustace dear.**
12   **EUSTACE: You're right, Clarinda. Perhaps she *would* fit in**
13   **our circle.**
14   **CLARINDA:** *(To PATSY)* **I'll tell you what it is. We want her**
15   **in our circle.**
16   **EUSTACE: Our sewing circle.**
17   **CLARINDA: We've heard she's Episcopalian, but that**
18   **won't matter. As long as they don't call themselves**
19   **Church of England anymore, we'll forgive them. Can**
20   **you imagine a *patriot* belonging to the Church of**
21   **England?** *(EUSTACE shakes her head vigorously.)* **I**
22   **think it's a terrible shame that an Episcopalian had**
23   **to be our first president. But at least it's better than a**
24   **Methodist or a Baptist. Won't those Methodist ladies**
25   **be jealous when they find out we got Martha**
26   **Washington to join our circle?!**
27   **PATSY: What church do you ladies represent?**
28   **EUSTACE: Well, really we don't represent anyone. We're**
29   **not officers.**
30   **CLARINDA: Be quiet, Eustace.** *(To PATSY)* **We are from the**
31   **Front Street Church located at Front and Bridge.**
32   **Our circle bears the proud and lofty name of "The**
33   **Front and Center Bridge Builders." Bridge Street**
34   **used to be known as Center Street, you know. But**

1 then I don't suppose you would know, coming from
2 Virginia and all.
3 **EUSTACE: Clarinda thought of the name all by herself.**
4 **Not one of the ladies had even considered it.**
5 **CLARINDA: We meet every other Tuesday in the church**
6 **parlors to tear bandages. We used to tear them for our**
7 **own soldiers, but now we've been sending them to**
8 **France. We've heard that Mrs. Washington tears a**
9 **straight bandage. I'm sure she'll fit right in.**
10 **EUSTACE:** *(Nods agreement.)* **Fit right in.**
11 **CLARINDA: I'm not sure, though.** *(EUSTACE immediately*
12 *switches from nodding yes to shaking her head no.*
13 *CLARINDA's voice drops to a stage whisper as if telling a*
14 *secret.)* **We've heard she's – dowdy.**
15 **PATSY:** *(Pretending to be shocked)* **Oh, no! What a terrible**
16 **thing! Do you suppose a dowdy would be accepted at**
17 **your circle?**
18 **CLARINDA: We'd have to warn them, I'm sure. If she just**
19 **walked in unannounced...why, you never know what**
20 **might happen. Someone might say something**
21 **unkind. But if they knew she was coming – if they**
22 **knew who she was, I'm sure they'd be careful not to**
23 **say anything until she was gone.**
24 **EUSTACE: We're sure they wouldn't say anything to her**
25 **face.**
26 **CLARINDA: All the ladies will realize what a terribly great**
27 **honor it is to have the wife of the president in our**
28 **circle. Why, we'll be the envy of every other circle in**
29 **town. Do you think she'll do it? Or will she stay with**
30 **those hoity-toity Episcopalians?**
31 **PATSY: I guess you'll have to ask her that question.** *(Calls*
32 *Off-stage.)* **Eleanor!** *(ELEANOR CUSTIS enters.)* **Eleanor,**
33 **will you entertain these ladies for a while? I have to**
34 **make some more arrangements for the reception.**

1   *(PATSY exits.)*
2   **ELEANOR: Yes, Ma'am.** *(She curtsies to MRS. VANDER-*
3   *HOOFEN and MRS. DINWIDDIE.)* **How do you do? I'm**
4   **Eleanor Custis, the president's granddaughter.**
5   **CLARINDA: Well, my, my, my! What an elegant little lady.**
6   **Very impressed, I'm sure, dearie. Aren't we, Eustace**
7   **dear?**
8   **EUSTACE:** *(Bobs her head.)* **Oh, yes, very impressed. We**
9   **didn't know the president had such a lovely grand-**
10 **daughter. We heard they were very plain.**
11 **ELEANOR:** *(Sits and smooths out her skirts.)* **Our grand-**
12 **parents have been very kind to my brother and me.**
13 **We have greatly enjoyed living with them here in**
14 **New York.**
15 **CLARINDA: I suppose it is nice. We've heard he lives like a**
16 **king with all those servants he brought from**
17 **Virginia. I can't imagine why he would keep one on**
18 **like that Patsy who met us at the door, though. She**
19 **seemed so dowdy for a rich house like this one.**
20 **EUSTACE:** *(Bobbing her head vigorously)* **Yes, dowdy to be**
21 **sure. Why do they keep her on?**
22 **ELEANOR: Patsy? A servant? You must be joking. That was**
23 **my grandmother, Martha Washington.** *(MRS. VANDER-*
24 *HOOFEN and MRS. DINWIDDIE flee in surprise and*
25 *embarrassment.)*
26
27
28
29
30
31
32
33
34

CHAPTER SIX

All the World's on Your Stage

Planning Your Setting

Jerusalem, Judea, in the days of Herod the King.

Thebes, Egypt, in the days of Queen Hatshepsut.

Athens, Greece, in the days of the apostle Paul.

Cape Town, South Africa, in the days of David Livingstone.

Shanghai, China, in the days of Hudson Taylor.

Washington, D. C., in the days of President Bill Clinton.

All of these exotic locales plus thousands more just like them can be recreated on the stage of any church in the world. Drama can bring the entire world into a church auditorium while at the same time providing insight for a congregation to gain a better view of the entire world. Barriers of time and place cease to exist when the writer sits down to create a sketch. It can take place in any locale and at any time, past, present or future.

Because most sketches take place in the chancel area with the rest of the service taking place directly afterward, usually no set (or only a very simple one) is used. Occasionally you may want to try something different.

Stage sets come in a variety of designs. They may be minutely realistic creations of the original place, or they may be only a suggestion of a locale through the creative use of lighting, color or symbolic set pieces. The writer does not need to determine what type of a set a director will ultimately choose to construct. In fact, sketches have been successful both when produced with a great variety of set designs or with none at all. What the writer must decide is where the protagonist lives, works and plays, and which one or two locations within the world of the protagonist would be the best location for the action to take place in the sketch.

A sketch will be easiest to produce if all of the action takes place in a single location. In the three to ten minutes of sketch action, there often isn't enough time to change locations. One set is also easier on the production budget, and for a sketch of a few minutes, this is a necessity. It will be easier to move if you decide to take the show on the road to other churches. It will help the action of the sketch move along quickly because there will not be long pauses for scene changes. If the location can be suggested by a single item such as a telephone booth, sofa, kitchen table, reception desk or set of barbells, your sketch will be even easier to stage.

There are creative ways to stage plays with multiple settings. A Readers Theatre approach where the sets are all in the mind of the audience has been used successfully when a story line calls for rapid movement from one location to another. A unit set, curtains, or different levels of platform with changes of lighting provides another approach to solving quick changes of scene. However, as a general rule, a writer should make every possible effort to write for a single location.

Be careful not to call for special effects which cannot be accomplished on the stage where your sketch will first be produced. A revolving stage, hydraulic lifts and trap doors will probably not be available in most church sanctuaries. Don't write a sketch that requires them, even if you have seen them used with tremendous effect in a professional theatre. Most proscenium theatres are equipped with fly lofts so that scenery pieces can be raised and lowered from above the stage. But church stages don't have fly lofts. Spectacle is an important ingredient in drama, but only if it is possible in the space available to a cast and crew.

The set description should be included in a paragraph just after the listing of the cast of characters. Write the description in terms of the characters, rather than in terms of a particular stage. Don't tell a director how to build the set. Describe the scene simply, remembering that it may look different in each production. The following scene description comes from my play *The Lazarus Plot,* published by Contemporary Drama Service.

The scene takes place in the house of Mary, Martha and Lazarus. It is a very plain, Hebrew home with stone walls and few furnishings. Two low benches provide the only furniture. A window near the front entrance looks out over a courtyard Stage Left. Another exit Stage Right leads into the cooking area where Martha prepares the lamb for the Passover dinner. A simple clay washing pot with a scrubbing rag and a sewing basket containing a robe in need of mending sit near the benches.

In this paragraph, not only is the scene description provided, but a prop list is included as well. For a longer play, you may want to list the properties separately, but in this case, with such a simple set, it was easier just to explain it all in one paragraph.

When choosing the setting for your play, you must keep in mind several factors. One of them is action. If your play portrays the stoning of Stephen, can you realistically ask the audience to believe that a stoning took place in Stephen's living room? If the action demands an outdoor setting, then decide how the entire play can be written to take place in front of the city gates. Since there was often an open-air market just outside the gates in biblical times, such a location suggests some great possibilities for dramatic action. Be sure that you create a set in which something can happen.

Another factor which should be considered is the use of your set as a metaphor for the theme of the play. A play about the Crucifixion could take place in the shop of a cross-builder. *Fire on the Sawdust Trail*, a play about the early revival campaigns of Evangelist Billy Sunday, uses a set which calls for a saloon and a Billy Sunday tabernacle to face each other across the town square like two boxers ready to duke it out. The conflict between the saloon and the tabernacle is visually evident from the set itself.

A third factor in choosing your setting should be its relationship to the sketch as a whole. What location would be the most logical one for the conflict you have envisioned to come to

71

a climax? Is this a place where the protagonist and antagonist would naturally meet? Will the characters you have created seem comfortable in this environment, or will they seem out of place? Is this the only environment where the unique events of your sketch could possibly happen? Would the story be different if it took place in some other location?

Scenes for contemporary sketches could include any location the people in your audience frequent. In fact, one way to obtain ideas for sketches is to imagine Bible characters in contemporary settings. Joseph in a health spa. Daniel in a state university dorm room. Mary and Martha at a garage sale. David and Goliath on a basketball court. King Saul in a television studio being interviewed by a political analyst. Paul on the road to the Super Bowl.

A set can also help actors who are limited in rehearsal time. A kitchen table can provide a surface where scripts could be available for quick reference out of sight of the audience. A newscaster holding sheets of copy from the wire services could conceal among them key lines from the sketch. The yellow pages in a telephone book could include yellow pages of script.

If your sketch takes place over a long length of time, your set should change as the sketch progresses. Furniture should be moved from place to place. What housewife leaves her furniture stationary year after year? Lighting should change to suggest different times of the day. Changes in temperature and precipitation should have their effect on outdoor scenes. If your scenes indicate such changes it will be much easier for your characters to suggest them as well.

All of these changes can be suggested very simply by a writer within the text of the sketch. Indications of exits and entrances, time, season of the year and the use of hand properties are appropriate stage directions to be included in the script. All of these will help the actors and director create a scene, a believable environment which enhances the action of the sketch.

If you are going to tour a sketch or use it as part of a longer service, you will want to keep the set as simple as possible. The following sketch can be performed with two chairs and a table as the only necessary set pieces. Its purpose would be to introduce a message or series of messages from the book of Micah.

Heroes

by Robert A. Allen

"I'll give you Larry Bird for
Magic Johnson."

CAST OF CHARACTERS

Ben

A junior-high boy.

Larry

Another junior-high boy.

PRODUCTION NOTES

Both boys should be dressed casually. The scene is Larry's
back yard. The boys have their trading cards spread out over a
picnic table. The time is the present.

1   BEN: I'll trade you two Patrick Ewings and a Scottie
2   Pippen.
3   LARRY: No deal! I'm not giving up *this* card.
4   BEN: A Shaquille O'Neill rookie card, an Isiah Thomas
5   and a David Robinson.
6   LARRY: You're wasting your time.
7   BEN: I thought we were here to trade.
8   LARRY: We are. But not for this card.
9   BEN: Well, what will you trade?
10 LARRY: I'll give you Larry Bird for Magic Johnson.
11 BEN: You want Magic? I'll give you two Magics for that card.
12 LARRY; Sorry. No way.
13 BEN: Three Magic Johnsons and a Kareem Abdul Jabbar.
14 LARRY: Nope!
15 BEN: You think he's that great, huh?
16 LARRY: I want to be just like him.
17 BEN: You want to be like him? Why?
18 LARRY: Well, he's on the best team.
19 BEN: The Bulls?
20 LARRY: Nope!
21 BEN: The Dream Team?
22 LARRY: Better than that.
23 BEN: Better than the Dream Team?
24 LARRY: Yup. And he knows how things are going to turn
25   out before they even get started.
26 BEN: What is he, some kind of prophet?
27 LARRY: Right.
28 BEN: So he shaves points and throws games and makes
29   big bucks?
30 LARRY: Nope! He goes by the book.
31 BEN: Three Magic Johnsons, two Patrick Ewings, a
32   Christian Laettner and a Julius Erving still in the
33   original wrapper.
34 LARRY: Not for the entire Dream Team.

1   BEN: You think he could beat them all?
2   LARRY: He already has something greater than gold, and
3   he's still in the minors.
4   BEN: There aren't any minors in basketball.
5   LARRY: Who said anything about basketball?
6   BEN: You said you wanted to be like...
7   LARRY: Micah!
8   BEN: Say what?
9   LARRY: I want to be like Micah, the prophet. He's my hero.
10   BEN: I'm glad I didn't offer you my Charles Barkley.
11
12
13
14
15
16
17
18
19
20
21
22
23
24
25
26
27
28
29
30
31
32
33
34

CHAPTER SEVEN

Words Are
for Speaking

Writing Dialog

The following scene takes place in front of a church on a Sunday morning after the worship service. The names have been protected to change the innocent. It is intended for production only by indigenous mime troupes in the outback of Australia. All other groups should apply for mental assistance before undertaking rehearsals of these lines.

PARISHIONER: How happy I am to be talking with my minister. Rev. R. Bishop, let me tell you what a privilege I consider it to be to have this opportunity to stop here at the doors of our lovely church to visit with you after the morning worship service.

BISHOP: Mary Parishioner, the privilege is all mine. I saw you sitting there in the seventeenth pew from the front with your husband Tom, your son Andy, your daughter Mary, your mother Mary and your grandmother Mary. Hello, Mrs. Turner.

PARISHIONER: Yes, Rev. Bishop, that's where we sit every Sunday to listen to your wonderful sermons, like the one this morning about the wise man who built his house on the rock. Is that Jennifer Bowers?

BISHOP: *(Turning to the audience)* I would really like to move Mary along. If I spend this much time talking to everyone coming out the door, my wife's pot roast will be charcoal. *(To MARY)* Thank you, Mary. I'm glad you enjoyed it. I'm sure you learned something from it. We get what we pay for, don't we?

PARISHIONER: You can say that again. Speaking of which, my daughter Mary is selling postcards to finance her trip around the world with her third-grade class. May we put you down for three dozen?

You might hear this conversation at a church door sometime, but if you do, don't build a sketch around that snippet of dialog. In fact, it should probably be nominated for the "Empty" Awards in the category of Worst Religious Dialog of the Ecumenical Age. If no such category exists, it merits the creation of one.

Stage dialog is not just conversation. It is not a means of having a three-point sermon preached by two people instead of one. Stage dialog exists to establish the mood of the sketch, reveal specifics concerning character and advance the plot line. It should also be easy for your actors to say and easy to memorize.

Look again at the disastrous dialog between Rev. Bishop and Mary Parishioner. If you read the selection aloud, the two characters sound alike. They use the same speech patterns, the same vocabulary and the same diction. Characters in good stage dialog should be distinguishable by what they are saying, even if the identifying name tag lines were removed.

Bishop and Parishioner are also repeating each other's names in almost every speech, something which doesn't happen in everyday conversation and sounds even worse on-stage than if it did happen on the street. Enough repetition and the effect will become humorous. The sketch *Patsy* which followed Chapter Six had two characters who constantly repeated each other's names with the purpose of making them sound ridiculous. Don't do it unless you want your characters to sound silly.

Another problem arises when they begin telling each other information which the other person already knows. Some writers think they need to do this for the sake of an audience.

That may be true if you are on radio, but the effect on-stage is to make your characters look like idiots. If Rev. Bishop has to tell Mary that she was sitting in a pew with her family, she must be extremely dense. If she has to tell him that he's at the door of his own church greeting people, he probably slept through his own sermon.

The dialog also includes totally useless information. Granted, when people are talking, they often greet others or recognize the presence of others. But in stage dialog, such recognition would immediately suggest that the person mentioned had some significance to the plot. Mrs. Turner and Jennifer Bowers exist only as names in passing. Mary also takes time to describe the setting, maligning the intelligence of the audience as well as her own.

Rev. Bishop's remarks to the audience, once a common technique of playwrights called the aside, is seldom used today except in a humorous way. It breaks the unspoken agreement between the actors and the audience that both of them will suspend belief during the course of the sketch and pretend that the events portrayed are really happening.

Both Rev. Bishop and Mary are wordy, using slightly varied phrases to repeat the same ideas. Good stage dialog should build on itself, with each additional sentence growing stronger in its effect, rather than weaker. It should be simple and economical.

The Purposes of Dialog

How can you write well? By checking every word you write to be certain it accomplishes one of the purposes of dialog.

1. Dialog should establish mood and atmosphere.

As the curtain opens to reveal your set, the audience finds themselves transported to another time and another place. What a shock results if those who people that "other world" talk as if they were in the wrong place. Social customs, ethnic practices, cultural and historical events, and economic realities should all color the speech of people who occupy a common environment.

A character in a sketch about Paul's experience on the road to Damascus might enter with this speech: "Caravan's late again. If Rome really wanted to do us a favor, they'd make the road from Jerusalem safe for travelers."

Before you start to write, do some reading. Books which provide insight into the manners and customs of the people among whom your play takes place will give you details concerning their environment, which can then color your dialog. Your actors should know what is going on in the world around them — not so they can give long speeches which reveal that knowledge, but in order to use the commonplace references which color everyone's speech. Or better yet, if possible, spend time with those you plan to write about. If you're writing about the homeless, volunteer at a shelter or soup kitchen. Your writing will be stronger and more authentic.

The mood of a scene can also be created by intentionally playing against the prevailing emotion. When writing a tragic scene, such as the stoning of Stephen, the tendency is to have characters share their emotions openly. All of Stephen's friends get together and cry as his body is carried in from the street. Such a scene can quickly become melodramatic. The scene would actually be stronger and more emotionally moving if the characters tried to hide their emotions for the purpose of encouraging one another to carry on the work Stephen had started. A comic scene will become funnier if the characters seem to be totally serious in what they are saying. When lines are written for actors which make them appear to be striving for laughs, the humor soon disappears.

2. Dialog should reveal personality.

You have already spent a great deal of time developing the characters who will people your sketch. As you start to write lines for them, be sure to choose words which show what those characters are like.

Vocabulary should be different for each speaker. Look at the educational level your character has achieved. Should he talk like a college graduate, or like someone with a third-grade education? Check their occupations. Are there particular words and phrases they they would use because of the work they do? A carpenter's analogies and comparisons would come from woodworking and a fisherman's would come from nets and boats and fish, while computer programmers talk bits and bytes and hard drives.

Is this character a strong, dominant personality? Then his language should intimidate others or even destroy them. Look at the social and economic status. Does your character sound like a servant or a fashionable lady? Would your audience know her approximate income just by listening to her talk?

Characters reveal themselves by the subjects they discuss. They talk about their interests, and they approach unfamiliar subjects in view of those interests. They reveal their political leanings, their religious views and their prejudices by their choice of words. But they also reveal themselves by the way they say things. A person's language can be self-confident or timid. One person will speak profusely without much thought while another will speak carefully, choosing each word with precision. A proud person might continually interrupt others, suggesting that what he has to say is more important.

As you listen to people and the way they talk, you will soon discover that conversations seldom take place in complete sentences. Pauses, incomplete thoughts, and dangling ideas characterize everyday speech. This is important to the writer, not because you want your actors to be incoherent, but because you want them to sound natural. The conversational norm should be the goal for stage dialog. Formal speech should be reserved for formal speaking occasions.

The best way to check dialog to see if it sounds conversational rather than formal is to read it aloud. If it sounds like written speech rather than spoken language, it will continue to sound that way even in the mouth of the most talented actor. Give your actors lines which will reveal their personalities rather than lines which will reveal the writer's views or interests or abilities. Your concern should not be with writing "good" speeches in the sense of being grammatically correct or even theologically proper. Your concern should be with writing lines which are appropriate to convey the thoughts, emotions and personality of the character speaking.

3. Dialog should advance the plot line.

Besides the obvious fact that words are necessary to tell your story, dialog should move the sketch along by the very way in which it is written. For example, long speeches tend to slow down the action of a play while short speeches increase action. Since drama is visual and depends on action to make its point, most lines of dialog should be short. Long speeches should be used to convey material which cannot be portrayed by action such as emotional states and thoughts. If a character has a great deal of material to share, break it up with questions, interjections and objections from the other characters on-stage.

Just as conflict is the basis for your plot, so conflict should be a basis for your dialog. Two people who both have the same opinion are not nearly as interesting as two people who disagree on a given topic. If you expect to maintain the interest of an audience, you cannot go for any great length of time with all of your characters in agreement. The conflict of the large plot must be evident in every scene.

Don't let your characters say everything they know in one speech. Instead have them share one idea at a time, giving the audience an opportunity to grasp that concept before another one is thrown at them. Remember that they are hearing these lines for the first time — they don't have them memorized. This doesn't mean that every speech should be short. It may take a character a long time to share one idea. But don't confuse your audience by jumping to a second topic within the speech.

Limiting the information given within a single speech will also aid your characters in sharing vital information several times without sounding repetitious. Since this is the first time an audience has heard the story in your sketch every vital piece of information must be repeated to be certain that everyone understands what is happening. That doesn't mean that you have one character simply share the fact three times with different people. Your technique should not be that obvious. Instead, use action to underscore what is being said. Use partial sentences, interruption and conflict to make it seem natural for people to finish unstated ideas or repeat what they were saying with greater force because it has been opposed.

Dialog also moves the plot along by preparing the audience for action yet to come. It is a good idea to mention characters who will soon be making an entrance in order to help the audience recognize them when they appear. At times, dialog will be necessary to let the audience know about actions which have taken place or are taking place off-stage. Exposition is necessary to establish the past and bring the audience up to the present. But all of these will be more effective if combined with actions taking place on-stage as your characters talk. Don't let your sketch become an exercise in eavesdropping. Your plot will not be advanced if your audience is simply listening to a long series of conversations.

4. Dialog should be easy on your actors.

Since you want the actors who produce your sketch to sound natural as they talk, you will need to write lines which are easy for those actors to say. If you find yourself stumbling as you read your work aloud, change the words. Certain sound combinations, alliterative words, internal rhyme or difficult pronunciations can all be problems in oral speech.

For the sake of your actors, dialog should be understandable. The player should be able to tell from the words themselves what emotion you intended to convey. If the words are capable of a variety of interpretations, add an adjective in parenthesis to clarify the interpretation. "Yes," for example, can be said sweetly, sarcastically, belligerently, condescendingly, submissively or a great variety of other ways. What you don't want to do is include in your stage directions such comments as "throwing her hands up in front of her face." Just give the desired effect and allow the actor to choose the best method of conveying that effect.

Dialog should also be easy to memorize. One way to make it easier for your actors is to write individual speeches which tie together into one continuous movement. Various techniques will help you do that. Try to repeat at least one word from the previous line in the new line. That will give the actor waiting to speak a cue as to which line is next. Even if a word cannot be repeated, be sure the same idea is the subject of the response. Some of the most difficult lines to learn are those where a character ignores what has just been said and introduces a completely new topic.

Questions and answers also provide cues which make memorization easier. At times, complete repetition of lines can be used, particularly in conflict situations where the repetition is a questioning of the other person's sincerity or source of information. Sometimes you can use progression, where one person begins a sentence and someone else concludes it. All of these techniques, when used without becoming obvious, will be a great aid to actors learning lines.

Remember that the main purpose of your dialog is to tell the story of your sketch. Not one of the rules given in this chapter is absolute; all of them have been broken by successful playwrights. But if you break enough of them in one sketch, you probably won't get a chance to go to your second opening.

Notice how the dialog reveals character, moves the plot line along and establishes the mood of the following sketch.

Friendship Evangelism?

by Robert A. Allen

"It's all the government's fault. Conrad says
they're subsidizing the apartments. Our tax
money is ruining our neighborhood!"

CAST OF CHARACTERS

Ferne

A middle-aged housewife and active member of the Ladies
Missionary Society at her church.

Elsie

A friend of Ferne's and a member of the same church.

PRODUCTION NOTES

The women should be dressed appropriately. The scene is
the kitchen of Ferne's house. Elsie has come over for coffee.

1 *AT RISE:* FERNE is looking out the window, obviously
2   disturbed over what she is seeing.
3

4 **ELSIE: Terrible, isn't it?**
5 **FERNE: Worse than that. I just didn't think it would ever**
6   **happen here.**
7 **ELSIE: I know. Alfred just shrugs and says it's happening**
8   **everywhere, so we'll just have to live with it.**
9 **FERNE: Isn't that just like a man?** *(FERNE leaves window*
10   *and sits across from ELSIE.)*
11 **ELSIE: I told him that if it happened to us, we'd have to**
12   **move.**
13 **FERNE: I don't even want to think about it. Guess who's**
14   **coming to visit?**
15 **ELSIE: Maude Gilbert. Sorry to spoil your surprise, but I**
16   **called the church office not more than five minutes**
17   **too late. You'll just have to have me over for tea so I**
18   **can visit with her.**
19 **FERNE: Absolutely. Her letters are so exciting I can't even**
20   **imagine what it will be like to have her sitting right**
21   **here at my own kitchen table.** *(ELSIE rises and moves*
22   *to window.)*
23 **ELSIE: It probably wouldn't be so bad if there were just**
24   **one. But you know they'll overrun the place.**
25 **FERNE: I know. We couldn't sell now even if we tried –**
26   **without taking a big loss, that is.**
27 **ELSIE: And so close to the church.**
28 **FERNE: Practically camped on our doorstep.** *(Shudders.)*
29   **Oooh.** *(ELSIE returns from window.)*
30 **ELSIE: Will you put her in the spare bedroom?**
31 **FERNE: We're giving her ours. Nothing but the best for**
32   **Maude Gilbert. Heaven knows what she's been**
33   **through the last thirty years. Probably been that long**
34   **since she slept in a good bed.**

1   **ELSIE:** What a sacrifice.

2   **FERNE:** Yes, sometimes I think...

3   **ELSIE:** No!

4   **FERNE:** Yes, I do. She's had such an opportunity to serve

5   God. If only... *(A beat)*

6   **ELSIE:** You know, I hate to admit it, but I really have a

7   terrible time keeping all our missionaries straight. Is

8   it India or Italy where Miss Gilbert has been all these

9   years? I read her prayer letters, but I've never been

10   good with details.

11   **FERNE:** Cambodia. Right through the middle of the war

12   and everything.

13   **ELSIE:** The war?

14   **FERNE:** Sure. The Vietnam War. It never ended, it just

15   moved to Cambodia.

16   **ELSIE:** Oh. Then I guess she'll really have some stories

17   to tell.

18   **FERNE:** Maude has gone through hell to see those people

19   brought to Christ.

20   **ELSIE:** What a woman. *(FERNE stands and looks out the*

21   *window.)*

22   **FERNE:** What a shame.

23   **ELSIE:** It will ruin the neighborhood, that's for certain.

24   **FERNE:** It's all the government's fault. Conrad says

25   they're subsidizing the apartments. Our tax money is

26   ruining our neighborhood! *(ELSIE joins her at the*

27   *window.)*

28   **ELSIE:** Where are they from? They all look alike to me.

29   **FERNE:** I'm not sure. Conrad calls them Hmongs.

30   **ELSIE:** Hmongs?

31   **FERNE:** They're refugees from somewhere. Maybe Maude

32   will know. We'll ask her when she arrives. Oh, it's so

33   exciting to meet someone who has had the opportu-

34   nity to be a real missionary.

CHAPTER EIGHT

Go Ahead!
Write It Down!

Preparing Your First Draft

Playwright John Ervine took a twenty-mile walk to increase his circulation and help him feel the emotional state of his characters before sitting down to write his play. Eugene O'Neill took early-morning swims in the ocean prior to writing. Robert Sherwood created the entire play in his mind before committing anything to paper. Arthur Sullivan of Gilbert and Sullivan fame often gave the cast their music at the last minute, sometimes just the night before the play opened.

Whatever the method of composition, there comes a time when the computer keys must be pressed or the pen must be applied to paper. Getting started is one of the most difficult tasks for any writer, but it is also the only path ever discovered which leads to the finish line.

Some people are just full of ideas for plays. As soon as they find out you write drama, they start to deluge you with them. But these people will never see their ideas performed unless someone else writes them down because they never take the time to put those ideas on paper. As you read this book, you have probably had many ideas which would benefit various groups within your church. Now is the time to flesh those ideas out and give them substance so that ultimately they can be brought to life on-stage.

Don't worry right now about method. Some writers create their characters first and start them talking. Others outline the entire sketch in a synopsis form. You may want to choose a title first, but if a title doesn't come, skip it and name the sketch later. Character names are important, but don't let choosing the names hinder you from writing the sketch — names can be changed at any time during your writing. Don't even worry about how your sketch will end. Even the best-planned endings have a way of changing as the sketch develops. Just start writing, knowing that a first draft is like puppy love — you learn some important lessons which will improve your next experience.

Choose an idea that interests you. If you have seen a need in your own life, a sketch on that theme will probably meet the needs in others as well. Ideas can come from anywhere. Your initial impetus may come from a topic such as patience or peace or helpfulness. There may be a complete story from Scripture, like the Good Samaritan or the manna in the wilderness, which catches your interest. Someone may ask a question in a Bible study class and give you an idea for a dramatic way to answer that question. You may be assigned a subject if you are working with a pastor or leader who has already chosen themes and wants drama to illustrate them. A missions theme for vacation Bible school or a series of sermons on the fruit of the Spirit would then provide your catalyst.

Whatever the topic, the manner in which you approach the theme will come from within you. A sketch should not just be a propaganda piece in dialog. It should be a unique viewpoint which challenges the listeners to consider their own attitudes and opinions toward a particular subject. If it brings about a change in those attitudes or opinions, so much the better.

What do you see as the biggest problems with contemporary Christianity? What are its strengths? How does your life compare to the lives of those people we meet in the Bible? How do their problems correspond to ours? What does the church of today have to offer to the world? What can the church learn from the world? Do you see the church as one of the "establishment" institutions in which the public has lost its trust? What can be done by the church to disprove such an attitude? Is spirituality today the same as it was in Bible times? What values should be shared by a civilized culture?

Once you have an idea or theme, start to develop a situation in which that idea will be tested. Remember that conflict is the basis for drama. Develop one character who places a high value on patience and another who wants immediate gratification and show the conflict which results. Create a character who ardently desires to live at peace with herself and invent situations where conflict with her own inner nature denies her that peace.

One approach which can help you get started is to take Bible stories and update them — that is, place them in a contemporary setting. One drama troupe took the parable of the rich fool (Luke 12:16-21) and retold it in terms of a modern businessman who makes his money in the futures market. The drama group at Wooddale Church set the story of Joseph and Potiphar's wife (Genesis 39) in a health spa.

Start a notebook or file in which you keep ideas for sketches. Observation, reading, listening and experience will all provide you with a wealth of ideas. Write them down and begin to think about them, then choose the one that interests you the most and start to write.

The "Suppose" Technique

Another method which can help you get started is the "suppose" technique. Joseph Kesselring used this method when he wrote *Arsenic and Old Lace*. "I got the idea for *Arsenic* by deliberately selecting my grandmother as a focal point and trying to imagine the most improbable thing she could possibly do" (Miller, J. William, *Modern Playwrights at Work*, Samuel French).

Consider the following situation. Wilson, a missionary, is warned by Mgobi that the witch doctor will place a curse on him if he enters a particular village to preach. Now start to suppose the developments which could arise from that situation. Supposing Mgobi is telling the truth, Wilson could believe him but refuse to admit it because he doesn't want Mgobi to think he fears the witch doctor. Or Wilson could think Mgobi is lying to keep him away from the village. He could even reason that the witch doctor has put Mgobi up to this in order to provoke a confrontation.

With each of those developments, you can again apply the supposing technique. Suppose that Wilson thinks the witch doctor is trying to provoke a confrontation. He could approach the witch doctor directly, go to the village in spite of the warning or question Mgobi further to try to determine the truth. Each of those developments would lead to another step in the plot.

Imagine the following situation. A girl hears a rumor that her best friend is pregnant. Now start to suppose the developments from that situation. If she believes the rumor, she could spread it to others without checking its truth. If she doesn't believe the rumor, she might try to sound out her friend without actually telling her what she has heard. Suppose she approached her friend directly about it and was told that the child was from God and that her friend was still a virgin? Then you would have the predicament Mary found herself in with her friends.

The "What If?" Technique

A similar technique which will aid in plot complications is the use of "what if?" What if young King Josiah decided to investigate reports of idol worship by disguising himself and going to one of the suspected worship sites? What if Lazarus had a friend who knew about the plan of the religious leaders to put him to death? What if a young man today was confronted with a temptation like Joseph faced with Potiphar's wife? What if a new bride lost her husband like Ruth did and suddenly had to choose between returning to live with unbelieving relatives or continuing to follow the faith of her new family?

The "what if?" technique applies to developing contemporary sketch ideas as well. What if a church buys a piece of property only to discover that it is the site of an Indian burial ground and their Native American neighbors are totally opposed to their building on that property? What if a girl enters a written sermon in a contest and wins, only to discover when invited to deliver the sermon orally that the sponsors of the contest thought she was a boy and have always limited the contest to males?

Don't speculate on "what if" Scripture were changed, such as what if Goliath had killed David, but use the technique to fill in the gaps of what the Bible doesn't tell. The basic idea for my play about Timothy, *The Hearts of the Fathers,* came from the question: What if Timothy's father was opposed to him traveling with the apostle Paul?

As you begin writing, you should have some idea what length you want your sketch to run. A five-minute sketch to be used during a church service will probably be about eight to ten typed, double-spaced pages, depending on how many stage directions you include and on how much rapid-fire dialog it contains. A one-act may be anywhere from ten to forty pages long. A full-length, two-hour play will run about ninety pages. Although your sketch length can be trimmed during the rewriting process, you will want to have a target length in mind as you start to write. In order to discover how fast your sketch is moving, read it aloud while walking around the room and time the pages.

Your script must make clear who is speaking, which lines are dialog and which are stage directions. The London format places the character name in the left-hand column. The New York format sets the character name in the center of the page, typed in capitals. Either format is acceptable. Choose the style which your actors find easiest to read, and be sure that you are consistent within your script.

ASSIGNMENT: DEVELOPING SKETCH IDEAS

A church drama troupe whose main function is to illustrate the weekly message themes through original sketches will need a great many ideas. They will need to explore the possibilities of both comedy and tragedy as well as adventure, romance, mystery, suspense, biography, myth, legend and maybe even science fiction. Allow your imagination a free rein when it comes to developing ideas.

You may want to form a committee to develop ideas for sketches. In that case, you should distribute your pastor's sermon themes at least a month in advance and ask each person on the committee to come up with an idea similar to those in this assignment. When the committee chooses an approach it wishes to take, each member could then be given a week to write a short sketch on that theme. At the next meeting, discuss all of the sketches which have been written and either choose the one which best illustrates the theme or take the best ideas from different sketches and do the final rewrite as a committee.

Even if you do work as a committee, you will find that someone must take the initiative to write the sketches. Committees are good for brainstorming and coming up with ideas and they are good for rewriting and improving already existing scripts, but the actual work of writing will usually be accomplished more successfully on an individual basis.

For this assignment, you will need to use your imagination. A list of one year's sermon topics with Scripture references has been provided. This is an actual list of one pastor's sermon themes for fifty weeks of Sunday messages. One possible idea for formulating a sketch follows each sermon topic for the first six months. Your assignment is to set your imagination to work and come up with methods of illustrating the final six months of the year through drama. Then choose the idea you like the best and start writing. Don't put it off any longer. Get to work! Write it down!

January

First Week: "Welcoming the King"   *Scripture: Psalm 24*

Sketch Idea: A group of people are planning a reception for an important guest. When he arrives, they kill him (see John 1:12).

Second Week: "New Year's Resolutions"   *Scripture: Psalm 101*

Sketch Idea: A man in a baseball uniform is telling a friend that he has resolved to practice diligently on his golf swing, his quarterback passes and his fly fishing technique. The friend suggests that resolutions about baseball might be more practical, but the man argues that since baseball is what he does for a living, those resolutions would be too hard to keep.

Third Week: "The Long-Suffering of God"   *Scripture: Psalm 107*

Sketch Idea: A man knocks on the door of a home and explains that he has come from the bank to foreclose on a mortgage. The homeowner begs for more time and is granted a one-year extension. Then he threatens to call the police because the bank shorted him $.50 on his last statement (see Matthew 18:21-35).

Fourth Week: "Try Praise" *Scripture: Psalm 146*

Sketch Idea: Adapt the Aesop's fable about the contest between the wind and the sun trying to get a man to take off his coat. The harder the wind blew, the more he pulled the coat around him. But when the sun shone, he removed it willingly.

Fifth Week: "A Memorial or a Memory?" *Scripture: Psalm 112*

Sketch Idea: Two people stand admiring a statue of a man. Neither one can remember what the person did, but they both agree that it is still a beautiful statue.

February

First Week: "Christ and the Tax Collector" *Scripture: Luke: 19:1-10*

Sketch Idea: A clerk at a hotel desk refuses to rent a room to a very short person. When pressed for a reason, the clerk explains that short people cannot be trusted, that they are inferior to those over 5'8", etc.

Second Week: "What to Do Till the King Comes" *Luke 19:11-27*

Sketch Idea: A father asks his son to wash the car and the boy refuses, but his brother volunteers to do the job. However, the son who refused decides to do it and the other brother forgets about his promise (see Matthew 21:28-32).

Third Week: "Tears for a City" *Scripture: Luke 19:41-48*

Sketch Idea: A daughter informs her mother that she is leaving home to live with her boyfriend who is into the drug scene. Her mother does not approve, but still assures the daughter that she cannot do anything which will make the mother stop loving her.

Fourth Week: "Sacrificers Needed"   *Scripture: Luke 21:1-4*

Sketch Idea: Adapt the old joke about the chicken and the pig who were asked to provide a ham and egg breakfast. For the chicken, it would be a contribution; but for the pig, it would be a sacrifice.

March

First Week: "Will You Be Ready?"   *Scripture: Luke 21:20-38*

Sketch Idea: A young man answers the phone and assures the party on the other end that he will be ready. Then he gathers his fishing gear and puts on his fishing hat and vest. When the doorbell rings, his bride enters in her wedding dress.

Second Week: "Fellowship With Christ" *Scripture: Luke 22:54-62*

Sketch Idea: A mother tries to have a serious conversation with her teenage daughter, but the only response she receives is clichéd phrases and nursery rhymes patterned after typical memorized prayers.

Third Week: "Christ and the Thieves"   *Scripture: Luke 23:39-43*

Sketch Idea: Adapt the Victor Hugo story about "The Bishop's Candlesticks."

Fourth Week: "The Basis of Faith"   *Scripture: Luke 24:8*

Sketch Idea: Two workmen try to remember the instructions their boss gave them for installing and lighting a gas stove. When they can't remember, they conclude that probably the actual words weren't that important anyway, as long as they were sincere.

April

First Week: "The Need for Power"   *Scripture: Acts 1:8*

Sketch Idea: Two men are trying to figure out why they can't get a power tool to work. They try everything except plugging it in to the electrical outlet.

Second Week: "Who Owns the Church?"   *Scripture: I Cor. 3:1-9*

Sketch Idea: A futuristic, galactic "People's Court" judge tries to determine who owns the universe as two lawyers argue their case for their respective clients — Paulco, Inc. and the Apollos Federation.

Third Week: "Overcoming Temptation"   *Scripture: Gal. 5:16*

Sketch Idea: Joe is approached by a seductress at the health spa and has to leave his warm-up jacket behind in order to get away (see Genesis 39:1-20). (This idea was used at Wooddale Church, Minneapolis, MN.)

Fourth Week: "Making Right Choices"   *Scripture: Phil. 1:9-11*

Sketch Idea: Two young ladies discuss their options for an upcoming dating event. One boy, named Henry, is particularly undesirable in their thinking. When he calls, the one who doesn't answer the phone rejoices, thinking her friend was chosen by Henry. Then the friend hands the phone to her, saying, "It's for you."

May

First Week: "Grow Up for God"   *Scripture: Phil. 3:10*

Sketch Idea: People who have worked with each other in an office for several years share the information that each has recently faced a death in the immediate family. They conclude that they never really knew each other before that.

Second Week: "Making the Most of Motherhood"

Scripture: Ex. 2:1-10

Sketch Idea: A husband and wife are discussing an edict by their government that each family will only be allowed to have one child. They already have a daughter, and the wife is pregnant again. She refuses to consider an abortion, and the two of them agree to have the child at home and hide him from the neighbors. "What will we call him?" asks the father. "Moses," she says.

Third Week: "Then Am I Strong"   *Scripture: Phil. 4:13*

Sketch Idea: Two boys are arguing about whether one of them can lift a very heavy set of barbells and carry them across the room. One says he can prove it by getting a man to help him. "You never said I had to carry them alone," he tells his friend.

Fourth Week: "Prayer Is Intercession"   *Scripture: I Tim. 2:1-7*

Sketch Idea: Adapt the historical/fictional incident concerning the wooing of Priscilla Mullen by John Alden as told in Henry Wadsworth Longfellow's *The Courtship of Miles Standish*.

Fifth Week: "Watch and Be Sober"   *Scripture: I Thess. 5:1-11*

Sketch Idea: A rancher waits at the train depot for a mail-order bride, a girl he plans to marry sight unseen (see Gen. 24:63-67).

June

First Week: "The God of the Impossible" *Scripture: Rom. 4:13-25*

Sketch Idea: Two children visit a candy store. One tells the other that he can choose anything he wants and have it without paying. The second child argues that this is impossible. "No, it isn't," answers the first child. "My father owns the store."

Second Week: "The Math of Love"   *Scripture: II Peter 1:5-7*

Sketch Idea: Adapt the story of Ruth leaving her family to follow her mother-in-law's faith (see Ruth). (Idea used in Wooddale Church, Minneapolis, MN.)

Third Week: "A Father's Prayer"   *Scripture: Judges 13:8*

Sketch Idea: A school counselor is advising a student concerning prospective careers. In the course of the conversation he asks, "Have you ever considered going into your father's business?" The student explains that he was adopted into a new family and doesn't really know what his father does. In response to the question, "Who is your new father?" he says, "God."

Fourth Week: "Giving and Taking Advice" *Scripture: James 3:13-18*

Sketch Idea: A woman listens closely to the advice of her doctor, then confides in a friend that she has no intention of taking his advice. She just goes to see him once a week because it feels so good to spend time in the hospital; she likes the sound of his voice, and her mother did the same thing every week.

July

First Week: "Happy Birthday, America"   *Scripture: Joshua 23:3-8*
Sketch Idea:

Second Week: "Is Your God Tired?"   *Scripture: Isaiah 40:27-31*
Sketch Idea:

Third Week: "Jesus and Children"   *Scripture: Mark 10:13-16*
Sketch Idea:

Fourth Week: "In His Image"   *Scripture: II Peter 1:2-4*
Sketch Idea:

Fifth Week: "The Biblical Basis for the Offering"

Scripture: I Cor. 16:1-3

Sketch Idea:

August

First Week: "Christ and the Fishermen"   *Scripture: Luke 5:1-11*
Sketch Idea:

Second Week: "Look Out for the Lion?   *Scripture: I Peter 5:6-11*
Sketch Idea:

Third Week: "Giving Our Children to God" *Scripture: Genesis 22*
Sketch Idea:

Fourth Week: "The Symbol of Our Resurrection"

Scripture: Col. 2:11-13
Sketch Idea:

September

First Week: "Don't Quit"   *Scripture: Psalm 78:9*
Sketch Idea:

Second Week: "Prescription for Revival?   *Scripture: Isaiah 57:15*
Sketch Idea:

Third Week: "Practical Revival"   *Scripture: Psalm 138*
Sketch Idea:

Fourth Week: "Perpetual Revival"   *Scripture: Acts 2:47*
Sketch Idea:

October

First Week: "Resisting Revival"   *Scripture: Acts 7:51*
Sketch Idea:

Second Week: "A Prayer for Revival"   *Scripture: Habakkuk 3:2*
Sketch Idea:

Third Week: "Nothing Can Destroy"   *Scripture: I Peter 1:1-5*
Sketch Idea:

Fourth Week: "God's School System"   *Scripture: I Peter 1:6-12*
Sketch Idea:

Fifth Week: "How to Live Like a Saint" *Scripture: I Peter 1:13-21*
Sketch Idea:

November

First Week: "The Miracle Book"   *Scripture: I Peter 1:22-25*
Sketch Idea:

Second Week: "Drink Your Milk"   *Scripture: I Peter 2:1-8*
Sketch Idea:

Third Week: "Living a Balanced Life in an Unbalanced World"
Scripture: I Peter 2:8-17
Sketch Idea:

Fourth Week: "It's Just Not Fair"   *Scripture: I Peter 2:18-25*
Sketch Idea:

December

First Week: "For Christ Is Born of Mary" *Scripture: Luke 1:26-38*
Sketch Idea:

Second Week: "What Think Ye of Christ?"   *Scripture: Mt. 22:42*
Sketch Idea:

Third Week: "God, My Father" *Scripture: Mt. 26:36-46*
Sketch Idea:

Fourth Week: "The Christmas Spirit of the Shepherds"

Scripture: Luke 2:15-20

Sketch Idea:

CHAPTER NINE

Give It a Sketch-Shine

Revising

You've finished your sketch and it's ready for production in Sunday's worship service, right? WRONG! The universal rule of every book ever published on writing drama (with a few exceptions) is this: Plays are not written, they are rewritten!

Rewriting your sketch is a must if you want it to be successful when produced for an audience. What you are really doing during this process is testing it before small audiences before exposing it to a large audience. You will be much more pleased with the reaction of the group if you have listened closely to the reaction of the individuals you select during the rewriting process.

The first step in rewriting is to give the completed manuscript to several people and ask them to read it and give you an honest evaluation. Choose these people carefully with specific considerations in mind. Ask someone you trust in the area of grammar to check your sentence construction, spelling and language mechanics. A knowledgeable Bible teacher, maybe a member of the pastoral staff, could check your theology. Someone involved in drama could read it and offer suggestions concerning the staging, characterizations and dialog. Another person who enjoys attending play performances could give you a reaction to the plot and emotion of the sketch.

You certainly don't need to make every change these people might suggest, but do be willing to listen closely to them. When you finish your first draft, you are too close to the sketch to see some of its obvious weaknesses, and you don't want to wait until you see it as part of a large audience to spot them.

When you have collected comments, hopefully written, from

each of those individuals, it is time to sit down and work your way through the sketch once again. Evaluate each suggestion carefully and make the changes you think will improve the script.

Next comes a private reading of the script. Invite several friends over for a meal with the understanding that they are going to help you by reading your sketch out loud. Don't spring it on them after they arrive unless you want them to turn down every future invitation to dinner they receive from you. As they read, listen and take notes. This time you are the audience, trying to imagine what this will sound like to those who will one day see it in production. Take special notice of lines which the readers stumble over. You may need to rewrite those for your actors. Listen to the flow of the sketch, asking yourself if it moves along at the pace you intended. Watch the faces of the reader to see if the emotions, humor and surprises of the sketch affect them as they read. One of the keys to having a sketch which an audience enjoys is writing a sketch which actors enjoy presenting.

Armed with your notes and your own reactions, do a second rewrite. Remember that criticism of a scene simply cues you to look for the reason for the dissatisfaction. It doesn't require you to make the changes the critic suggests. Pay special attention to the development of the conflict and crisis. Be sure your character voices don't change during the course of the sketch. Even though main characters develop and change some aspect of their belief structure as a result of conflict, they should still sound the same at the end of the sketch. Vocabulary, grammar, pacing, dialect and sentence structure should still identify them as the same person. One way to check this is to read all of the speeches of one character from the beginning of the sketch to the end. As you do that, revise for consistency.

The final step in rewriting is to have the sketch produced. If you are writing a sketch for your church, you may want actors to perform it for a Sunday school class or small Bible study group a week or two before you schedule it for a major service. This will give you one more chance to make final changes which become obvious only during rehearsals or in front of an audience. Attend both the rehearsals and the performance and take notes on your

own reactions, those of the actors and most importar
reactions of the audience. This will help you sharpen the
strengthen the climax and focus the conflict and conclu ... ui
your sketch.

Rewrite Check List

During the rewriting process, check each of the following
items.

1. Does the theme of the sketch emerge clearly? Does the
audience understand the message you intended for them to learn?

2. Does the opening of the sketch introduce all of the major
characters? Are the character names distinct and the personalities varied enough so that the audience doesn't confuse them
with each other?

3. Does the sketch start with action and develop by
continued action? Have off-stage actions been described which
could more effectively be brought on-stage?

4. Does the sketch include scenes or dialog which are not
necessary to the development of the plot?

5. Does the sketch leave out any scenes which are necessary
to the development of the plot? Have you expected too much of
the audience, assuming they will possess background knowledge which may, in fact, be lacking?

6. Do your main characters have the most lines? Are they
on-stage most of the time? Do they face the greatest conflicts and
resolve the greatest crises?

7. Does the audience recognize your protagonist? Do they
know which character deserves their support and sympathy?

8. Is your dialog easy to say? Do the actors stumble over
sound combinations and gasp for breath at the end of long
sentences?

9. Could some of the dialog be rewritten as action? Are
speeches too long, conveying more than one idea at a time?

10. Have you constantly repeated character names? Do the
characters tell each other things the other person already knows?

11. Is your set simple? Could the costumes be made without great expense?

12. Is the manuscript clean? No misspelled words, typing errors or omitted lines?

13. Have you maintained a consistent format throughout the manuscript?

14. If needed, is there time for actors to make costume changes called for during the sketch? Is there time for them to complete off-stage actions which the script claims they have accomplished?

15. Is the title interesting and informative concerning the content of the sketch?

16. Could the sketch be shortened by eliminating a long expository passage at the beginning and jumping right into the action?

17. Have you written all of the dialog you expect the actors to say, or are there repeated instructions to "ad-lib"?

18. Does the sketch build throughout to the largest conflict and conclusion at the end?

19. Have you numbered every page so a director can quickly give directions to the cast?

20. Is there an event which brings about a transformation in the leading character?

21. Does the mood remain consistent? Is the humor integrated or obtrusive? Have you written a comedy and then attempted to bring it to a dramatic conclusion? Have you written a drama and then given it a comedic conclusion which will disappoint the audience? (A good example of this would be the worn-out technique of having a character wake up at the end to discover it was all a dream.)

22. Have you limited your number of characters to only those necessary for this sketch? Do you have on-stage characters who say almost nothing? Do you have those who never seem to come alive?

23. Are your entrances and exits strong? Do main characters

have good exit lines? Have you helped your audience to antici-pate the arrival of major characters?

24. Does the sketch involve numerous shifts in time and place, making it difficult to produce technically? Will the time and place changes you include be obvious to the audience even if they don't read the program?

25. Have you created a protagonist who is consciously striving to achieve a definite goal? Does the audience know what the protagonist wants?

26. Does the audience see the protagonist struggling to achieve those goals? Does the sketch show rather than tell?

27. Are the conflicts and obstacles faced by the protagonist realistic? Does the audience leave saying the story just wasn't believable?

28. Have you resorted to miracles or the appearance of long-lost rich relatives to solve conflict? Does the solution to the conflict come from the development of the characters within the story? Do you disappoint the audience by an obviously contrived ending? Is it necessary for a narrator to step in and explain every-thing at the end?

29. Does the sketch come to a definite conclusion? Do the characters leave the stage with strong words or actions? Is the audience satisfied that the protagonist has either achieved victory or been transformed by defeat?

Always remember the three "Thou shalt nots" that charac-terize good drama:

Thou shalt not preach, but teach.

Thou shalt not tell, but show.

Thou shalt not lecture, but entertain.

(Anonymous)

ASSIGNMENT: MOSES AND THE ROCK

This script, written by a Sunday school teacher for presen-tation by her class, was sent to me for evaluation and rewriting. Her story idea was original and significant, but the development of the theme quickly became strangled by problems. One of the major problems she faced concerned the actors available to her. Many of her students came from unchurched families. They received little encouragement from home in the memorization of lines. Although she felt that only two of her students were capable of handling major parts, she wanted everyone to be in the play, so there had to be parts for twelve children. The second casting limitation came from the fact that every student in the class was a boy. Using that information and the suggestions in this chapter, do your own rewrite and give it a sketch-shine. If you are not able to make numerous improvements, you'd better read the chapter over again.

Moses and the Rock
Scene 1

Mother waking up boys. Starts mixing batter in a bowl.

Mother: Jacob, Benjamin, time to get up and gather the wood.

Jacob: Oh, Mother, why do we need wood when it is so hot?

Benjamin: Don't you want to eat mother's delicious loaves for supper? You know she must have a fire to cook them on.

Jacob: But it is so hot.

Mother: Jacob, you know how we had to work in Egypt. Slaves! Every day we had to go and work for no pay. Jehovah has delivered us.

Benjamin: Moses says it is a land flowing with milk and honey.

Jacob: I sure hope it isn't so hot. Moses doesn't have to go find firewood. Let's go.

Scene 2

Men all gathered around. Moses trying to quiet them.

Men: Our children and wives are getting hungry. How are we going to feed them?

1st man: Would to God we had died by the hand of the Lord in the land of Egypt.

2nd man: We sat by the flesh pots and ate bread until we were full.

3rd man: Now we are in this wilderness and have nothing to eat. Are you going to kill all of us with hunger?

Moses: I will go before the Lord and plead for you. Remember how great and powerful the Lord is who delivered us from Egypt? Moses exits, kneels and prays. Men exit.

Mother: Come sit down and have a freshly baked cake. How did the meeting go? Did Moses know what we are going to do?

Man: He is going to plead before the Lord for us.

Mother: God has delivered us from Egypt. Surely he will not let us die in the wilderness. We are his people. The meal barrel is almost empty. Moses says we will have our land. We must have faith and trust God to provide for us.

Man: Yes, we must trust Jehovah, just as Abraham did.

Mother: Oh, yes. God told Abraham to take Isaac and go to Mt. Moriah and sacrifice him. Then Jehovah sent a ram to take Isaac's place. Jehovah could easily fill a barrel of meal.

Man: Call the boys, let us pray, and bring the Torah.

Scene 3

Spotlight on Moses kneeling in prayer. He looks up.

Voice: Moses, behold I will rain bread from heaven for you. And the people shall go out and gather a certain rate every day that I may prove them whether they will walk in my law or not. And it shall come to pass that on the sixth day they shall prepare that which they bring in and it shall be twice as much as they gather daily. I have heard the murmurings of the children of Israel. Speak unto them, saying, "At even, you shall eat flesh, and in the morning, ye shall be filled with bread, and ye shall know that I am the Lord your God."

Scene 4

Lights up slowly on day scene. Mother, Father and boys

getting up.

Jacob: (Eyes wide looking all around the ground.) Benjamin, Benjamin, look at the ground. Mother! Father!

All people gather around looking at ground, all talking at once.

All: What is it? What is it?

Moses: This is the bread which the Lord hath given you to eat. This is what the Lord has commanded. Gather an omer for every man, woman and child. Let no man leave of it till the morning.

Everyone gets a pot and starts to gather.

Benjamin: I knew God would provide. See how he answers our prayers? We are his children. God has given us the cloud and the pillar of fire, and last night, quail to eat, and this morning, manna. Jacob, are you gathering or eating?

Jacob: I have to see what it tastes like. It is like a wafer made with honey. This is pretty good, Benjamin. Try some.

Benjamin: There is enough for every man, woman and child to have an omer. We'd better get busy. Moses said it will melt when the hot sun comes out.

Mother: It has been a wonderful day.

Man: Yes, Jehovah has provided once again.

Suggestions for Improvement

One answer for this teacher's casting problems would be to confine the main action of the play to a family. She could play the part of the mother herself, and the two students who could memorize well would be the sons. Those three would then carry most of the dialog. The rest of the class would represent Moses and the children of Israel. These parts would be exciting even without great amounts of dialog because of the action involved. Moses would carry a staff and lead the people, taste the manna and pray. The children of Israel would complain, gather the manna and eat it. All the boys would enjoy those roles.

The format definitely needs attention. Stage directions must be immediately recognizable rather than being confused with dialog. Choose a format and follow it consistently. You'll be amazed at how much more readable the manuscript will become.

An even greater problem with the script concerns character development. The action of the story springs from the hunger faced by the family, but the sketch still needs conflict within the family in order to sustain audience interest.

To produce conflict, change Benjamin to a cooperative son and Jacob to a complainer. Rewriting every line of dialog with just those two characteristics in mind makes the boys into something more than identical twins. It also produces tension between Jacob and his mother which can then be resolved at the end of the sketch.

The dialog also calls out to be rewritten. Remember, dialog is not ordinary speech. Raymond Hull in *How to Write a Play* calls it "speech concentrated and directed." The three areas where dialog must be concentrated are in revealing character, creating atmosphere and advancing the plot. The words spoken by Benjamin, Jacob and their mother must demonstrate their strained relationship, convince the audience this is taking place in the wilderness and reveal the basic problem they face — could God really meet their need for food? Look back through your rewritten dialog and ask yourself if each speech accomplishes one of those three purposes.

A sketch-shine would also certainly do something about the conclusion. The scriptural conclusion is of course evident — God will meet their need by providing the manna. But now we have a conflict between family members to resolve as well. The audience is wondering if Jacob has learned to trust God rather than complain. This is the conflict which makes the lesson practical in the lives of the students and their audience.

In order to provide a satisfying conclusion, you will need to make the lesson which Jacob learned practical to him. All of the children of Israel were hungry, and all were satisfied by God's provision. Jacob needs a unique lesson. One method of providing that would be to give him additional complaints besides hunger. He might have to gather firewood during the hot wilderness days and maybe he had run out of honey to put on his bread. He would blame these additional problems on his mother and her God.

Then when Moses announces that the manna must be gathered, Jacob could conclude that he still had another hot job to perform. But Moses says that the manna must be gathered early, before the sun melts it, so Jacob's complaint about the hot sun is satisfied. His other complaint disappears when Benjamin tastes the manna and announces that it tastes just like honey. Jacob could then realize that God's concern included him personally and that he was able to provide for Jacob's every need.

Your rewrite will correct other weaknesses in addition to these. Follow the same process with your own sketches, and they'll be much better when you finish.

CHAPTER TEN

In Search of the Perfect Fit

Tailoring Drama to Suit Your Needs

Drama in the church, once limited to the obligatory Christmas pageant, has come of age. You can serve any aspect of your church ministry by contributing sketches which will evangelize, edify, exhort and entertain. The secret to success will be in tailor-making your sketches to fit the occasion and audience. Fulfill the expectations of leadership, actors and audience, and your talents will be in constant demand.

Drama to Fit the Pastor

Many pastors plan their sermons a year or more in advance. While I was pastoring, my practice was to set aside time during vacation to outline a preaching plan for the next twelve months. Titles, texts and themes are usually known by a preacher long before he starts specific preparation of a message.

In order to fit your drama to the needs of your pastor, you should approach him with the idea of illustrating a series of messages with short drama pieces. Ask for the titles and themes of messages at least twelve months in the future and be willing to write without any promise that your scripts will actually be performed. If drama has not been used in your church previously in this fashion, he will need to see the completed scripts before giving his blessing to the project. *Heroes*, the sketch following Chapter Seven, would be a good example of drama written to introduce a series of messages — in that case, on the book of Micah.

If you let your interest in drama be known, a pastor may himself initiate the process. Leith Anderson of Wooddale Church in Minneapolis invited a drama committee to illustrate an upcoming series on the fruit of the Spirit. Five people planned and wrote four- to five-minute scripts to correspond with each of his messages. The sketches were presented during the worship service as an integral part of the preparation for the morning message.

All of the sketches were written as a committee. (Willow Creek also uses this technique.) The members would meet and talk about the theme, then each member would develop a skit concept which they would bring back to the next meeting. At that meeting, a final idea would be discussed and one person would be assigned to write the dialog. Finally, the committee would rewrite and approve the last draft. Pastor Anderson's entire series on the fruit of the Spirit received emphasis from these four- to five-minute dramas.

After you have received initial approval from the pastoral staff, announce auditions or simply contact six to eight individuals who would be willing to form a drama troupe. These persons should be willing to meet for at least two hours on a weekly basis, but they must be aware that those involved in a sketch for Sunday may have an additional responsibility for more rehearsal. As a matter of courtesy, it would be good to go over your list of troupe members with the pastor, but it is you as the leader who will have the ultimate responsibility to the church. Steve Pederson says that no church should start a drama ministry "without the key persons identified and confirmed by those responsible in the church." He warns against starting "with only well-intentioned people who don't have strong enough leadership skills or drama experience."

As a drama team, write your first three or four sketches and submit them to the pastor for him to read. Invite him to attend the Sunday school class or other gathering where you try out the sketch during the rewriting process as explained in Chapter Ten. Remain open to any suggestions he might offer. After all, it is his sermon you are trying to illustrate.

Suggest to the pastor a target date for your first performance, and obtain his approval for the sketch which will be used on that day. Then get to work on rehearsals and determine to perform to the best of your ability and for the glory of God. A strong performance with positive audience reaction will be the best possible means of assuring yourselves of additional opportunities in the weeks to come.

If your pastor is hesitant to share sermon topics several weeks in advance, go through the same process but use themes of your own choosing. You will find that certain preaching themes occur on a regular basis. Use the ideas from this list or from themes suggested previously in the book.

Prayer

Service

Missions

Comfort

Stewardship

Word of God

Faithfulness

Forgiveness

Christian growth

Humility

Salvation

Spiritual gifts

Drama to Fit the Budget

For many years, the Jesus People Church in Minneapolis presented an annual version of *A Christian Christmas Carol* in an old theatre building which they had converted to their meeting place. The cast numbered in the hundreds, the costuming and lighting were exquisite and the response terrific. Word of Life has traveled with their version of the *Passion Play*. The Master Arts Company of Grand Rapids, Michigan, presented a staged version of *The Book of Job* in Byzantine mosaic makeup and costumes. The city of Oberammergau, Germany, produces its *Passion Play* once every ten years, involving the entire community and attracting thousands of visitors from around the world.

But what about the church which doesn't have the resources to mount such a production? You can write your drama in a way which will make it easy on the budget of your church to bring it to production.

The first thing you will want to do is to keep the cast small. For a sketch, use three to six characters. A full-length production could include up to a dozen, but try to avoid anything over that. Larger casts are not only more difficult to direct, they immediately demand a larger budget in terms of costuming, makeup and staging requirements.

If possible, write the sketch to be done in contemporary costuming. Authentic period costuming is very impressive and if your sketch takes place in biblical times or some other historic period, you should seek to costume it as accurately as possible. But if budget is a great concern, then a contemporary time frame will save you considerable time and money.

Give the characters guidelines and allow them to develop their own costumes. Or assign a parent or other responsible adult to create a costume for each person. Volunteers will have to be given specific directions in order to maintain a semblance of unity in the design of the sketch, but they can save you a great deal of money as compared to renting costumes or hiring someone to construct them.

Another budget buster can be elaborate, multiple sets. It is very impressive for the curtain to rise and reveal a scene which recreates Da Vinci's *Last Supper* in every detail. But if your sketch moves from there to the Garden of Gethsemane and then to Golgotha and the garden tomb, you are asking for a major outlay of funds just for the backdrops and stage props. Your sketch will be simplest to produce if you limit yourself to a single setting.

You might also consider writing a sketch which can be produced with no set at all. Short sketches to be used in a worship setting must almost always be of this variety. A desk and a chair could suggest an office, or a table and a couch could represent a living room. Those items could be placed on-stage and then removed quickly following the sketch in order not to distract from the rest of the service.

Drama to Fit Your Acting Troupe

If your church has already been using scripts from Contemporary Drama Service and other publishers, or even if your scripts are the first they will use, you probably have some idea of who are your potential actors. Maybe an acting troupe already exists for whom you are writing. Perhaps you started the team yourself through auditions. Maybe you have just looked around and observed some people whom you think would enjoy this aspect of ministry. Whoever your actors are, you will want to tailor-make your drama for them.

The same principles apply to writing a sketch for a particular group as they would to choosing a published sketch for an organized acting troupe. The better you know the actors who will perform the work, the better job you can do in writing a vehicle which maximizes their strengths and minimizes their weaknesses.

Your first consideration must always be the worth of the theme. Are you asking these people to expend time and effort on a project which will be worthwhile? If your focus has been on communicating the truth of the Gospel, then you can be sure the theme is of great worth. But you also need to consider the fact that a great subject can be treated in a trite and unworthy manner. The value of your sketch will be determined not just by its theme, but also by its theatricality. Some sketches read well but don't act well. To act well, a sketch must involve conflict and deal with human problems with which the audience can identify. If the characters simply talk about those problems, the sketch will not be as effective as if they act out the overcoming of the obstacles to their success in the sight of the audience. Does the sketch have value both theologically and dramatically?

You must also ask if the script has a unique, individual approach to the subject. Don't be satisfied with mediocrity or with trying to imitate a program which has made some other church successful. This is one of the great advantages of writing your own materials: being able to inject your own unique outlook into the dramatic ministry. Books have suggested that there are only sixteen to twenty plots in all of literature, whether fiction or drama. But there are endless, unique variations to those plots. As a writer, you need to read extensively so you will know what has already been done. Then use your God-given imagination to develop a unique approach which will grip the hearts of your listeners and challenge them with your theme.

One of the characteristics of great literature is universality. Shakespeare's and Molière's plays continue being produced years after the death of their authors because they concern human qualities such as pride, avarice, loyalty, love and hate which arouse common emotions in audiences today. You certainly don't have to compete with Shakespeare, but at the same time, you should strive to write a sketch which will give your actors a chance to affect a major portion of those attending the production. Choose themes which because of their univer- sality will find acceptance by your audience.

You will also do your actors a great favor if you give them a sketch which challenges the audience before whom they are acting. Even when the major purpose of the sketch is entertain- ment, an audience should be left with something to think about. This should not be understood as an excuse for turning a sermon into dialog and calling it a sketch. But the playwright should always strive for dramatic impact, facing issues with honesty and forthrightness and fearlessly tackling the faults and foibles of mankind. Humor in particular can be an effective tool for chal- lenging people in areas which they would not otherwise face. Provide your actors with the means of changing people's lives.

When you have worked with a group of actors for any length of time, you will want to start writing sketches which challenge them in their dramatic development. They need sketches with characters who are more than just stereotypes or imitations of popular TV personages. There will be a tendency to try to reproduce imitations of your successes or the successes of others. If one of your actresses does an excellent job creating the role of an indulgent grandmother, you will probably at least think about writing another sketch where she can be a grand-mother again. Don't do it. Give her and the rest of your actors the opportunity to develop characters which stretch their talents. Portray your characters honestly, developing them well through strongly motivated action. An actor who sees a part as a chal-lenge will exert greater effort to play that part well.

You should also be sure to write sketches which can be cast with the people you have available. If you have several strong actresses but no one who really qualifies as a leading man (a common predicament for church drama groups), write a sketch which emphasizes female roles. An audience will find great humor in a preteen trying to play the part of a senior citizen, but if you don't want your sketch to be humorous, write it for the ages of your actors. An outstanding actor or actress can play a part which varies extensively from his or her own age, but even then, the audience tends to focus on the incongruity of the situ-ation. If they find too much incongruity in the cast selection, they will fail to get involved in the story line.

For the sake of your acting troupe, it is important to provide variety in your sketches. You may feel that you are best at writing humor, or tragedy, or melodrama. But your actors need to develop by involvement in various categories of drama, and your audience needs to be kept guessing as to what is coming next. Do yourself and them a favor by challenging yourself to write a variety of sketches.

You will also want to write sketches which can be quickly committed to memory. Some people memorize faster than others, but all of your players will appreciate conversational speech and connected dialog.

Rehearsal time is always a problem for nonprofessional groups. One suggestion is to meet during the Sunday school hour, have a short lesson from one of your team members and then use the rest of the time for rehearsal. This would be a good way to conduct a final dress rehearsal on the Sunday when your sketch will be performed, but it probably will not be adequate for your entire rehearsal schedule.

Your group should plan to meet at least three hours a week

in order to prepare a four- to five-minute sketch. Do them a favor by starting on time and remaining focused on the work you are doing. A typical rehearsal would include: a short physical warm-up using improvisation or theatre games available in many acting books, a read-through of the sketch to be performed, discussion of the interpretation of the lines, adequate time for blocking so everyone is comfortable with the movement, a break for individual memorization, and enough complete run-throughs so the entire production seems polished.

Drama to Fit the Church Program

Gone, hopefully forever, are the days when the only play a church ever saw was the pageant presented at the annual Sunday school Christmas program. Allowing for some creativity, which you as a playwright will supply, drama can be used in any aspect of the church program. Consider the following possibilities to get your creative juices flowing:

Sermon starters	Baptisms
Discussion groups	Weddings
Youth meetings	Thanksgiving
Junior church	New Year's Day
Sunday school	Sanctity of Life Sunday
Ladies' retreats	Contests
Couples' retreats	Fund-raisers
Missionary conferences	Dinner theatre
Christmas	Stewardship Sunday
Easter	Discipleship classes
Mother's Day	President's Day
Father's Day	Street theatre
Birthdays	Rest home services
Ordinations	Budget kick-offs
Anniversaries	Choir practice
Valentine's banquets	Teachers' meetings
Independence Day	Deacons' meetings
Church picnics	Honor banquets
Children's Day	Vacation Bible school

Day camp	Prayer meeting
Summer camp	Graduation exercises
Youth missions trips	Promotion Sunday

The possibilities are endless. There is a place for drama in your church, even if you don't start out incorporating sketches as part of your weekly worship services. Write that script and make drama a part of your church programs.

Drama to Fit Your Congregation

Not every church is ready for a drama ministry which participates in each service. You and your church leadership will be the best judges of how rapidly you want to move toward that goal. Perhaps once a month will be a more feasible goal at first. But you can help your church see the possibilities for preparing the mind for the preaching of the Word of God through drama.

As you are planning your initial sketch or series of sketches, ask yourself what types of drama will be most familiar to your congregation. Are they accustomed to missions themes, Christmas pageants or children's programs and Easter celebrations which contain elements of drama? Perhaps your first productions could build around those familiar elements.

Be certain that you have the full support of the pastoral staff for your endeavor, and if at all possible, have your pastor announce several weeks in advance that a drama troupe has been organized and will perform during the service on your target date.

Remember to analyze your audience. You will want to be certain that your sketch does not offend their theological views or their sense of what is appropriate in worship. Be certain that your sketch does not patronize them or cause specific individuals or groups within the congregation to feel that they have been singled out for ridicule. There is no way you can change lives unless you first of all obtain a hearing.

How can you convince a congregation totally unaccustomed to drama in the church that it deserves a valid place as a means of ministry? The best way is to purchase or write an outstanding script which will challenge them spiritually and move them emotionally. Then produce it in the most professional manner possible, trusting God to help people see the impact it has on their own lives and the lives of others around them. Once a church experiences the impact which drama can bring to the ministry, they will be pleading with you just as this book has: DON'T GIVE UP THE SCRIPT.

Sketch Collection
Introduction

These sketches introduce today's church shopper to churches we sincerely hope do not exist. If, perchance, you do visit one of them somewhere other than on-stage, don't blame us — we tried to warn you.

Each sketch runs about ten minutes, long enough to incite you to consider the spiritual condition of your own church-going, but not long enough (hopefully) to incite you to hang the author in effigy. Individual production notes are also included. Use them if they are valuable to you, ignore them if you have a better way to engage your audience in a humorous self-evaluation.

Church shoppers need all the help they can get as they face the smorgasbord of spiritual sustenance which will be offered in the twenty-first century. Provide them with a church shopper's guide to the universal church by producing these plays, and they will be eternally grateful. Or at least they will get a good laugh (we hope).

First Church of Automation

by Robert A. Allen

"I am so excited. The First Church
of Automation has been installed
right here in my living room!"

Do we attend church to hear what we want to hear, or to
hear what God wants to communicate to us?

CAST OF CHARACTERS

Phil Apew
The average church-goer

Micah Jordan
A sports prophet

Bella Donna
An arts spokesperson

Billy Friday
An old-time revivalist

Siggy Freud
A 'good advice' columnist

Bubbles
A stand-up comedian

Two voices in the audience

PROPS

Remote control, stool, and five television monitors on tall, square stands — large enough for a person to hide behind. The monitors may be as simple as cardboard boxes with a screen cut out and power, volume, and channel buttons painted on them.

PRODUCTION NOTES

The play takes place in the display booth of the First Church of Automation, a new concept in church which is being marketed to the church-going public. Phil Apew, who represents the church congregation, "channel surfs" his way through a trial run of the new, automated system. Micah Jordan, Bella Donna, Billy Friday, Siggy Freud and Bubbles' faces are visible through the television monitors. As Phil points his remote control at each screen in turn, each character offers a short snippet of talk before Phil changes the channel again. All characters freeze when not speaking, coming alive only when Phil points the remote control at them.

1   *(MICAH JORDAN, BELLA DONNA, BILLY FRIDAY, SIGGY*
2   *FREUD and BUBBLES are in place behind their TV moni-*
3   *tors. PHIL APEW sits on a stool in front of the screens.)*
4 **PHIL APEW: I am so excited. The First Church of**
5   **Automation has been installed right here in my living**
6   **room. Now I can have church any time I want it, any**
7   **way I want it. And best of all, there are no offerings.**
8   **Of course, I have to send a large check to Heavenly**
9   **Inter-Cable once a month, but...let's see what chan-**
10   **nels I have.** *(PHIL points his remote control at MICAH*
11   *JORDAN's screen.)*
12 **MICAH JORDAN: This is Micah Jordan bringing you the**
13   **latest in sports religion. The competition was fierce**
14   **today as David played in the courts of Saul. Young**
15   **David is still basking in his victory over the heavy-**
16   **weight contender Goliath after which the roar of his**
17   **triumph could be heard throughout the land.** *(PHIL*
18   *points remote control at BELLA DONNA's screen.)*
19 **BELLA DONNA: With an appreciation of all that is beau-**
20   **tiful in religion, this is Bella Donna bringing you**
21   ***Lifestyles of the Meek and Merciful.* Come with me as**
22   **we visit the summer home of John the Baptist on the**
23   **banks of the Jordan River and partake with him of a**
24   **meal of gastronomic delight: succulent locust and...**
25   *(PHIL points remote control at BILLY FRIDAY's screen.)*
26 **BILLY FRIDAY: What are you doing in front of that TV set?**
27   **This is Billy Friday here, and I'm here to tell you that**
28   **nothing good ever came from watching TV. So turn**
29   **off that set and get on the phone. Call all your friends**
30   **and neighbors and tell them to tune in and listen to**
31   **me – Billy...** *(PHIL points remote control at SIGGY*
32   *FREUD's screen.)*
33 **SIGGY FREUD: Are you ill, distracted, wretched, depressed**
34   **and miserable? Siggy Freud here with a promise.**

1 Watch me regularly and you'll hear from those who
2 are far worse off than you. Today: Religious parents
3 with demon-oppressed children. *(PHIL points remote*
4 *control at BUBBLES' screen.)*
5 BUBBLES: When you have a name like Bubbles, no one
6 ever takes you seriously. You know, they think you're
7 an airhead, an overinflated drip. But that's all right
8 because I'm in good company. Think about it. How
9 seriously did they take Noah? "Say folks, there's a low
10 pressure system headed down out of Turkey, and I
11 think we're in for a real squall." No one has taken
12 weather forecasting seriously ever since then.
13 PHIL APEW: Isn't this great? Church in any style I want.
14 And it's supposed to be interactive too. Say, how about
15 helping me go for a test run? You give me an idea for
16 an announcement you'd like to hear, and we'll see
17 what happens.
18 VOICE 1: Ladies Missionary Circle.
19 PHIL APEW: All right. Let's see what happens to the
20 Ladies Missionary Circle in the First Church of
21 Automation. *(PHIL points the remote control at SIGGY*
22 *FREUD's screen.)*
23 SIGGY FREUD: Today on Siggy: We'll be talking with
24 unusual church mothers who have overcome unbe-
25 lievable odds to attend monthly meetings designed to
26 help them interface with the challenge of worldwide
27 evangelism. *(PHIL points remote control at BILLY*
28 *FRIDAY's screen.)*
29 BILLY FRIDAY: All right, men. You're the head of the
30 home, so get your bod off that couch and do the
31 dishes so the little lady can get to her missionary
32 meeting. *(PHIL points remote control at BELLA*
33 *DONNA's screen.)*
34 BELLA DONNA: Like a symphony of the soul, the ladies of

1   **First Church will blend their multitudinal talents**
2   **into an orchestral Church Aid Concert for the less**
3   **fortunate of Eastern Europe.** *(PHIL points remote*
4   *control at MICAH JORDAN's screen.)*
5   **MICAH JORDAN: Don't miss the action as the women of**
6   **the church take the field in tourney action against**
7   **the team of the evil empire and go to bat for the guys**
8   **at the bottom of the heap.** *(PHIL points remote control*
9   *at BUBBLES' screen.)*
10   **BUBBLES: The Ladies Missionary Circle will meet this**
11   **week to make tallow candles for the refugees in**
12   **Eastern Europe. Each lady is requested to bring her**
13   **own fat for rendering.**
14   **PHIL APEW: Hey, that was great. Are you ready for the**
15   **sermon? How about one of you suggesting a topic?**
16   **VOICE 2: Tithing!**
17   **PHIL APEW: Who was that, the head of the finance**
18   **committee?**
19   **VOICE 1: Televangelists!**
20   **PHIL APEW:** *(Sarcastically)* **That's a topic that should bring**
21   **real conviction to the members of this congregation.**
22   **VOICE 2: Love.**
23   **PHIL APEW: As a noun or a verb? Doesn't matter? All right.**
24   **Let's give love a try.** *(PHIL points the remote control at*
25   *BILLY FRIDAY's screen.)*
26   **BILLY FRIDAY: There's no love in the world today. Don't let**
27   **anyone kid you. The liberals talk about love, but they**
28   **don't know what love is. Movie stars talk about love,**
29   **but they wouldn't recognize...** *(PHIL points remote*
30   *control at BELLA DONNA's screen.)*
31   **BELLA DONNA: ... a beautiful flower with smell as well as**
32   **shape. Love germinates even in the dry wasteland of a**
33   **lonely human spirit, but blossoms only...** *(PHIL points*
34   *remote control at MICAH JORDAN's screen.)*

1   **MICAH JORDAN: ... in the end zone. Pick up that football**
2   **of love and fire it in the direction of a receiver, a**
3   **fellow church member, a teammate who can tuck it**
4   **away and carry it...** *(PHIL points remote control at*
5   *BUBBLES' screen.)*
6   **BUBBLES ...in the mouth like a sour pickle. Laughter is**
7   **good for the soul. When I was growing up in church,**
8   **laughing on Sunday was the quickest way to lose your**
9   **religion. One day in church, the deacons spilled an**
10   **entire Communion tray down the front of Mabel**
11   **Schnickelgruber's white dress and she...** *(PHIL points*
12   *remote control at SIGGY FREUD's screen.)*
13   **SIGGY FREUD: ...walked right down the aisle and gave that**
14   **preacher a big hug. That's what this world needs is**
15   **more hugs. Hug your friends. Hug your enemies. Hug...**
16   *(PHIL points remote control at BILLY FRIDAY's screen.)*
17   **BILLY FRIDAY: ...your *TV Guide*. Real love is what the world**
18   **needs. None of this namby-pamby, two-faced, weasel-**
19   **eyed, cotton-pickin' puppy love the media gives us.**
20   **Puppy love never led to anything but a dog's life. What**
21   **Hollywood knows about love would fit inside...** *(PHIL*
22   *points remote control at MICAH JORDAN's screen.)*
23   **MICAH JORDAN: ...a hockey puck. Zinging around that**
24   **rink, caroming off one player and then another,**
25   **uniting everyone in a common effort – that's what love**
26   **should do to the church. The church is a team. Don't**
27   **just yell your love from the sidelines, show love with**
28   **your hockey stick, show love with...** *(PHIL points remote*
29   *control at BELLA DONNA's screen.)*
30   **BELLA DONNA: ...the essence of skunk. This woman actu-**
31   **ally thought the smell of skunk was a perfume. She**
32   **was able to love the unlovely. How wonderful it would**
33   **be if, like that woman, we could discover love for**
34   **unlovely people like...** *(PHIL points remote control at*

1   *BUBBLES' screen.)*
2   **BUBBLES:** ...**pianists and choir directors. I went to a church**
3   **once that didn't have a choir. The preacher said he**
4   **wasn't about to have anyone talking behind his back.**
5   **So the choir said, fine...** *(PHIL points remote control at*
6   *SIGGY FREUD's screen.)*
7   **SIGGY FREUD:** ...**we don't need hot air balloons. We can't**
8   **survive if we just drift aimlessly off into space. We**
9   **need each other. We need the church. We need love.**
10   **We need...** *(PHIL points remote control at MICAH*
11   *JORDAN's screen.)*
12   **MICAH JORDAN:** ...**a left-handed pitcher for the church**
13   **softball team. That's the practical outworking of love –**
14   **getting involved in the church's sports program. If you**
15   **really love one another you will...** *(PHIL points the*
16   *remote control at BILLY FRIDAY's screen.)*
17   **BILLY FRIDAY:** ...**put all those pinko, commie-sympa-**
18   **thizing, molly-coddling Hollywood types into prison**
19   **where they belong. If you really want to show love, you**
20   **will...** *(PHIL points remote control at BUBBLES' screen.)*
21   **BUBBLES:** ...**realize that we are in grave danger spiritually**
22   **when we lost the ability to laugh at ourselves. When I**
23   **see how foolish I am...** *(PHIL points remote control at*
24   *BELLA DONNA's screen.)*
25   **BELLA DONNA:** ...**I shout "Hallelujah." Give me another**
26   **grain of sorrow so I can encase it in love and produce**
27   **another pearl. Love is a many-splendored thing. Love**
28   **makes the world go around. Love...** *(PHIL points remote*
29   *control at SIGGY FREUD's screen.)*
30   **SIGGY FREUD:** ...**has regular weekly meetings. Please join**
31   **us for our newest support group: Loving the**
32   **Unlovable, or How to Be Your Own Best Friend.**
33   **PHIL APEW: Isn't that exciting? That's just about the most**
34   **exciting sermon I've heard since the church dinner**

where the preacher mistook Tabasco sauce for tomato juice. He didn't just preach fire and brimstone, he breathed it. And say, feel free to stop by and visit anytime. You won't find me going anywhere else for spiritual refreshment now that I have the First Church of Automation.

First Church of Fame

by Robert A. Allen

"Welcome to another exciting edition of
Church Styles of the Rich and Famous
with your sports prophet, Micah Jordan."

Do we want a church to be recognized for its temporal achievements or for its eternal faith?

CAST OF CHARACTERS

Rev. Hornblower
Pastor of the First Church of Fame

Micah Jordan
The sports prophet

Misty Optic
A color commentator

PROPS

Three chairs, three lapel microphones.

PRODUCTION NOTES

First Church of Fame is written as a radio program which is being recorded before a live audience. The characters should sit in comfortable chairs with lapel microphones attached.

1   MICAH JORDAN: You're listening to station K-N-O-W,
2   where we're always "in the know" regarding church
3   news – you know? Welcome to another exciting
4   edition of *Church Styles of the Rich and Famous* with
5   your sports prophet, Micah Jordan. I am here in the
6   spacious auditorium of the First Church of Fame
7   along with our color commentator, Misty Optic.
8   MISTY OPTIC: And what an exciting day it is, Micah.
9   Before this day is over, we expect the First Church of
10   Fame to become the very first church ever to be
11   inducted into the Superchurch Hall of Fame.
12   MICAH JORDAN: That's right, Misty. And with us as well is
13   that future hall-of-famer himself, Rev. Hornblower,
14   who within just a few minutes will know whether his
15   is indeed the biggest name in all Christendom. But
16   before we talk to Rev. Hornblower, could you give us a
17   little background on this prestigious award, Misty?
18   MISTY OPTIC: Certainly, Micah. During the past two
19   decades of phenomenal church growth, unsubstan-
20   tiated claims such as "fastest-growing" and "largest"
21   and "most spiritual" have proliferated. So *Church
22   Styles of the Rich and Famous* hired me to keep
23   statistics.
24   MICAH JORDAN: And what a job you have done.
25   MISTY OPTIC: Thank you, Micah. I've always thought it a
26   shame that you could pick up the Sunday paper and
27   find the games pitched, saves, and won-lost records of
28   the major leaguers, but no records from our churches.
29   MICAH JORDAN: But now you have changed all that, and
30   today we are going to hear the results of your work.
31   Rev. Hornblower, how will achieving this milestone
32   help your ministry?
33   REV. HORNBLOWER: Tremendously, Micah. I've got a lot
34   of good years left in my preaching career, and I just

1   want to share them with the world. I feel as good

2   today as I did the day I preached my first sermon.

3   MISTY OPTIC: June 10, 1961. You were given the largest

4   signing bonus of your entire seminary class, as I recall.

5   MICAH JORDAN: And you were voted rookie Preacher of

6   the Year by the Pulpit Press Writers Association.

7   REV. HORNBLOWER: Yes, that was one of my first

8   projects – the Pulpit Press Writers Association. Still

9   going strong, too.

10   MISTY OPTIC: That first year you preached one hundred

11   forty-eight complete sermons with an ERA of 2.26.

12   MICAH JORDAN: You might need to explain ERA for some

13   of our listeners who are less familiar with the termi-

14   nology of preaching statistics.

15   MISTY OPTIC: Certainly. ERA stands for Exegetical

16   Research Average. It is obtained by dividing the

17   number of references to the original languages into

18   the overall length of the sermon and multiplying by

19   the number of main points.

20   MICAH JORDAN: And I see that Rev. Hornblower's is very

21   low.

22   MISTY OPTIC: Absolutely. But he goes off the end of the

23   scale on his RBIs.

24   MICAH JORDAN: RBIs?

25   MISTY OPTIC: Relevant Biblical Illustrations. That first

26   year Rev. Hornblower averaged an amazing eleven

27   RBIs per sermon. The highest in the entire National

28   Church League.

29   MICAH JORDAN: Wow! And you've been at this for over

30   thirty years now, Rev Hornblower?

31   REV. HORNBLOWER: That's right. The last three years

32   here at First Church I've served as the Designated

33   Preacher. I don't get around to home base as often as

34   I once did, but then I don't have to. We've added a

1   young rookie to the staff who runs to home for me –
2   my designated runner, if you will.
3   MICAH JORDAN: I'll bet that really takes a load off your
4   feet. Well, Misty, what else can you tell us about this
5   amazing church?
6   MISTY OPTIC: Maybe I should just run through some of
7   these statistics for you. Win-loss record: two hundred
8   eighty-seven to seventy-three.
9   MICAH JORDAN: Two hundred eighty-seven wins and
10   seventy-three losses?
11   MISTY OPTIC: Right. Three hundred sixty monthly busi-
12   ness meetings in thirty years, and only seventy-three
13   losses. That is some record. Here's another one: on-
14   base percentage, .501.
15   REV. HORNBLOWER: That's one I'm particularly proud
16   of. The entire congregation felt my ideas were off-
17   base less than half the time.
18   MICAH JORDAN: How about attendance records?
19   MISTY OPTIC: This auditorium has been sold out weeks
20   in advance of every pulpit appearance. And appear-
21   ances in other arenas are a sure hit too. Other
22   churches are assured of a record attendance when
23   Rev. Hornblower is scheduled to visit. In fact, he once
24   preached to the largest group assembled since the
25   crossing of the Red Sea.
26   REV. HORNBLOWER: Counting both the Israelites *and*
27   the Egyptians.
28   MICAH JORDAN: Amazing. To think that even the
29   Egyptians would come to hear you preach. Well, here
30   we are, just waiting for word from the Superchurch
31   Hall of Fame on the induction of its first-ever
32   honoree. Misty, what else can you tell us about this
33   amazing church?
34   MISTY OPTIC: Well, there are some really unusual

1   records which have been set here at First Church of
2   Fame.
3   MICAH JORDAN: Unusual records?
4   MISTY OPTIC: Right. For example, this church holds the
5   record for the most money raised in a single offering.
6   MICAH JORDAN: Really? How did you do it, Rev.
7   Hornblower?
8   REV. HORNBLOWER: It wasn't that hard. We just had
9   everyone save up their offerings for an entire year
10   and give it all on one day. Made headlines in every
11   major newspaper across the nation, though.
12   MICAH JORDAN: I bet it did.
13   MISTY OPTIC: And the church holds the record for the
14   largest living Easter egg ever displayed inside a
15   church auditorium.
16   REV. HORNBLOWER: Yes, last year the living Easter egg
17   grew so large that there wasn't room for anyone to
18   come see it. So we simply televised the program and
19   let people watch it in the comfort of their own homes.
20   MICAH JORDAN: Well, I must say you have set some
21   awesome records here at First Church of Fame. Is
22   there any category, Misty, where this church does not
23   emerge as the pacesetter for all churches worldwide?
24   MISTY OPTIC: As a matter of fact, there is one, but only
25   one.
26   MICAH JORDAN: And what is that?
27   MISTY OPTIC: Faith. There's a church in Central America
28   which doesn't have a full-time pastor or a choir or
29   even a building. But they really hit home in the faith
30   category.
31   REV. HORNBLOWER: But how does that affect their
32   standing in the overall Superchurch Hall of Fame
33   scoring percentages?
34   MISTY OPTIC: Very little, actually. It seems that no one

1   places a great deal of value on faith these days. It's so
2   much easier to evaluate what we can see.
3   MICAH JORDAN: Absolutely. Why, I don't know of any way
4   we *could* evaluate a church's faith, so why try?
5   REV. HORNBLOWER: My sentiments exactly. Let's
6   compare ourselves in the areas that *really* count.
7   MICAH JORDAN: Well, folks, we have it. I have just been
8   informed over the hidden speaker in my ear that First
9   Church of Fame has been unanimously inducted into
10   the Superchurch Hall of Fame.
11   MISTY OPTIC: Congratulations, Rev. Hornblower. And
12   what do you have to say on this prestigious occasion?
13   REV. HORNBLOWER: It's just so wonderful to know that
14   no matter where you come from, once you get there,
15   there you are.
16   MICAH JORDAN: Beautiful, Rev. Hornblower, just beau-
17   tiful. And now that you have won the championship,
18   what are you going to do?
19   REV. HORNBLOWER: Do you need to ask? I'm going to
20   Disneyland.
21
22
23
24
25
26
27
28
29
30
31
32
33
34

First Church of Offense

by Robert A. Allen

"I just don't think it's nice to invade their territory.
I mean, let's face it, that end of the field belongs to them."

Do we go to church to advance the case of Christ or simply to defend our territory?

CAST OF CHARACTERS

Dr. A. D. Vance

Iry Seaver

Count Downem

Boomer Wrange

PRODUCTION NOTES

The First Church of Offense takes place on the field of life. Players can wear full uniforms or use just helmets or football jerseys to suggest that they all belong to the same team. The team members can be played by either men or women.

1   **DR. VANCE: All right, team. Huddle up!** *(Instead of gath-*
2   *ering around DR. VANCE, the others huddle together*
3   *away from him.)* **What's the delay? This church has a**
4   **goal to strive for.**
5   **IRY SEAVER: Just a minute, Dr. Vance. We think it's time**
6   **for some negotiations.**
7   **DR. VANCE: Negotiations? We're in the middle of a game**
8   **and you want to negotiate with our opponents?**
9   **COUNT DOWNEM: Not with them. With you.**
10   **BOOMER WRANGE: That's right! We don't like the way**
11   **this game is going.**
12   **DR. VANCE: Neither do I! So what do you expect the other**
13   **team to do while we're negotiating?**
14   **IRY SEAVER: They'll wait. We have the ball.**
15   **BOOMER WRANGE: We do? Sure. We have the ball. They'll**
16   **wait.**
17   **DR. VANCE:** *(Sarcastically)* **I bet they will. I wouldn't trust**
18   **them as far as I could carry the entire team.**
19   **COUNT DOWNEM: That's what we want to talk to you about.**
20   **DR. VANCE: About not trusting them?**
21   **BOOMER WRANGE: About carrying the entire team?**
22   **IRY SEAVER: No, about having the ball.**
23   **DR. VANCE: About having the ball? That's the point of this**
24   **entire endeavor. We're trying to reach the goal. We're**
25   **the offensive team.**
26   **COUNT DOWNEM: We don't want to be offensive.**
27   **DR. VANCE: You what?**
28   **BOOMER WRANGE: We don't want to carry the ball.**
29   **DR. VANCE: Wait a pigskin-pickin' minute. Let me get this**
30   **right. You all belong to the First Church of Offense,**
31   **right?**
32   **ALL: Right.**
33   **DR. VANCE: You're all members of our team and not the**
34   **other team, right?**

1   ALL: Right.

2   DR. VANCE: But you don't want to carry the ball?

3   ALL: Right!

4   BOOMER WRANGE: They might laugh at us.

5   COUNT DOWNEM: They might persecute us.

6   BOOMER WRANGE: Yeah! A guy persecuted me once. He
7   sat on my head and persecuted it right into the ground.

8   IRY SEAVER: I just don't think it's nice to invade their
9   territory. I mean, let's face it, that end of the field
10   belongs to them.

11   DR. VANCE: And you think they'll leave us alone if we stay
12   on our end of the field?

13   COUNT DOWNEM: It's worth a try.

14   BOOMER WRANGE: You could still throw the ball to us and
15   we could have a great time running around in circles.

16   IRY SEAVER: Besides, they get mad at us when we try to
17   advance the ball, and I really don't like to make
18   people upset.

19   DR. VANCE: But what about our goal? What about
20   reaching our goal?

21   IRY SEAVER: Well, we thought maybe the goal could be
22   redefined.

23   COUNT DOWNEM: Right! Instead of all this emphasis on
24   winning, we thought maybe we could define our goal
25   as "having a happy day while playing."

26   DR. VANCE: Having a happy day?

27   BOOMER WRANGE: Hey, we could paint happy faces on
28   the back of our helmets.

29   DR. VANCE: Sure, then our opponents wouldn't know we
30   were running from them when they chase us off the
31   field. This is ridiculous.

32   COUNT DOWNEM: You're not giving it a fair chance.
33   Think of how our attitudes would improve with a
34   happiness huddle.

1   DR. VANCE: They'll push us right back to our end zone.

2   IRY SEAVER: But we'll be able to say, "We're happy with

3   the territory we're able to control."

4   DR. VANCE: They'll take the ball away.

5   COUNT DOWNEM: And we'll say, "We're so happy with this

6   opportunity to defend what we stand for."

7   DR. VANCE: So defense is all right, but not offense?

8   IRY SEAVER: Oh, yes, we have to have defense.

9   BOOMER WRANGE: Defense doesn't make them mad.

10   They expect that from us.

11 COUNT DOWNEM: It's really just the offensive part of the

12   game we don't like. I mean, it's so much trouble

13   moving the ball forward.

14 BOOMER WRANGE: I don't like to leave all my friends and

15   run out there into enemy country. Why, a person

16   could get hurt out there.

17 IRY SEAVER: Right! Let's just stay where we are. We can

18   have our happiness huddle, toss the ball around the

19   circle, wave at our friends in the other huddle and go

20   home.

21 COUNT DOWNEM: And that way, no one will get hurt.

22 DR. VANCE: And who is going to tell the coach about this

23   new goal?

24 IRY SEAVER: Well, we thought maybe...

25 COUNT DOWNEM: You know him so much better...

26 BOOMER WRANGE: He wouldn't believe it if we told him.

27 DR. VANCE: You're wrong there. I think he already knows.

28 IRY SEAVER: What do you mean?

29 DR. VANCE: Well, I heard him ask the owner for some

30   laborers to send into the field. I didn't understand

31   until I got out here, but whatever you three are, you

32   are not laborers.

33 BOOMER WRANGE: So maybe we'll be replaced so we

34   don't have to play offense?

1   **DR. VANCE:** I doubt it. The laborers are few, according to
2   the coach.
3   **IRY SEAVER:** So we have to play offense?
4   **DR. VANCE:** That's why we're here. *(COUNT, BOOMER and*
5   *IRY move away and huddle up. After some whispering,*
6   *they return to DR. VANCE.)*
7   **IRY SEAVER:** We have another suggestion.
8   **DR. VANCE:** Now what?
9   **COUNT DOWNEM:** You take the ball. Hike it to yourself.
10   Throw yourself a pass. Run out and catch it and see if
11   you can reach the goal.
12   **DR. VANCE:** And you?
13   **IRY SEAVER:** We'll have our happiness huddle.
14   **BOOMER WRANGE:** And we'll cheer you on! Rah, rah, siss,
15   boom, bah!
16   **COUNT DOWNEM:** What do you think?
17   **DR. VANCE:** I think that whatever you three are, you are
18   not football players.
19
20
21
22
23
24
25
26
27
28
29
30
31
32
33
34

First Church of Promotion

by Robert A. Allen

"Promoting God. What a revolutionary concept.
I wonder if that could be developed into
an advertising campaign?"

Do we meet to promote our church or to promote the Lord?

CAST OF CHARACTERS

Dr. Will B. Known

A. Gent

Eddie Cate

Rush Dipace

PROPS

Three chairs and an easel to display three pieces of poster board with the following ad slogans written on them:

1) Sunday Slam, Rumble With the Reverend.

2) Will B. and Friends.

3) Fit for the Master's Use.

PRODUCTION NOTES

The play takes in the conference room of the First Church of Promotion where Dr. Will B. Known has invited A. Gent, representative of Celestial Promotions, Inc., to make his advertising presentation.

1   (*DR. WILL B. KNOWN, EDDIE CATE and RUSH DIPACE*
2   *are sitting. A. GENT is standing by his easel with the*
3   *three ad posters. The first poster should be turned over to*
4   *start.*)
5   **DR. WILL B. KNOWN:** Recognition, Mr. Gent, recognition
6   is what we are seeking. Your agency has been hired
7   for one purpose and one purpose alone, and that's to
8   make this the First Church of Promotion.
9   **A. GENT:** Dr. Will B. Known, I promise you that Celestial
10   Promotions, Inc. will do everything in its power to
11   bring you satisfaction.
12   **DR. WILL B. KNOWN:** That's why we hired you. I've had
13   numerous colleagues tell me that your ideas are out
14   of this world.
15   **EDDIE CATE:** Ethereal!
16   **RUSH DIPACE:** Heavenly!
17   **A. GENT:** Well, you know our motto: Ads by Celestial Are
18   Extra-Terrestrial.
19   **DR. WILL B. KNOWN:** Yes. Well, you've met Eddie Cate and
20   Rush Dipace, so let's get started.
21   **A. GENT:** Very well. Let's begin by having you tell me what
22   you see as your church's greatest asset.
23   **DR. WILL B. KNOWN:** Well, my sermons, maybe?
24   **EDDIE CATE:** They *are* great. And they get greater every
25   week. Sometimes we don't get home until after one
26   o'clock.
27   **DR. WILL B. KNOWN:** My wife says they're immortal.
28   **RUSH DIPACE:** That's right. I heard her say that just last
29   Sunday. "Will," she said, "I know your sermons are
30   immortal, but do they have to be eternal?"
31   **EDDIE CATE:** That's good, Rush.
32   **A. GENT:** To be up front with you, Dr. Will B. Known,
33   churches just aren't recognized for good preaching
34   these days. There are too many tremendous speakers

1   around, politicians and news commentators and

2   professional boxers...

3 **DR. WILL B. KNOWN:** Boxers?

4 **A. GENT:** Well, maybe not boxers. But no one goes to

5   church to hear preaching anymore. Now if you were

6   to try some professional wrestling techniques...

7 **RUSH DIPACE:** You want Dr. Will B. Known to go into the

8   ring?

9 **EDDIE CATE:** That would attract a crowd.

10 **A. GENT:** No, no. Just their advertising technique.

11   Something like: *(A. GENT reveals his first advertising*

12   *scheme.)* "Sunday Slam. Rumble With the Reverend."

13 **RUSH DIPACE:** I like that.

14 **EDDIE CATE:** Has a nice *ring* to it.

15 **DR. WILL B. KNOWN:** All right, if you two are so smart –

16   what do you think is our greatest asset?

17 **EDDIE CATE:** Our educational program, of course.

18   Sunday school, the Memorize-a-Verse Club...

19 **RUSH DIPACE:** And aerobics – Sweating With the Saints.

20 **A. GENT:** I hate to disappoint you, but the Memorize-a-

21   Verse Club went out with bell-bottom pants, and no

22   one uses the term Sunday *school* anymore. School

23   has such a negative connotation with children.

24 **DR. WILL BE. KNOWN:** Then what should we call it? *(A.*

25   *GENT reveals his second poster.)*

26 **A. GENT:** How about "Will B. and Friends"?

27 **RUSH DIPACE:** Sure. We could dress him up in a purple

28   outfit and sing...

29 **RUSH/EDDIE:** *(Singing to the tune of "This Old Man")* "I love

30   you, you love me/We're a happy family..."

31 **DR. WILL BE. KNOWN:** No, I don't think I like that idea.

32 **A. GENT:** Then maybe we should go with the aerobics

33   idea. *(A. GENT reveals his next poster.)* "Fit for the

34   Master's Use."

1   RUSH DIPACE: We could exercise to the tune of "Joshua
2   *Fit* the Battle of Jericho."
3   DR. WILL B. KNOWN: Right! Or "How Firm a Foundation."
4   EDDIE CATE: "Day Is Dieting in the West."
5   DR. WILL B. KNOWN: But what about those who just can't
6   seem to thin down?
7   A. GENT: I guess you could close each session by singing,
8   "There a Wideness in God's Mercy."
9   DR. WILL B. KNOWN: No, I just don't think the aerobics
10   approach fits our church. We don't really want to
11   promote thinning.
12   RUSH DIPACE: Maybe we should just promote our unity. It
13   worked for the early church.
14   EDDIE CATE: But we don't have any unity. We can't even
15   agree on a simple advertising slogan.
16   DR. WILL B. KNOWN: Besides, they didn't use unity to
17   promote their church, they were united because they
18   were all promoting God. *(Pause)*
19   A. GENT: Promoting God. What a revolutionary concept. I
20   wonder if that could be developed into an advertising
21   campaign? I could make my fortune.
22   DR. WILL B. KNOWN: You'll have to give me credit for the
23   idea. I'll settle for fifty percent of the gross.
24   RUSH DIPACE: I brought up the seed thought of unity. I'm
25   going to hold out for twenty percent.
26   EDDIE CATE: I was here when it happened. How about
27   five percent?
28   A. GENT: That only leaves twenty-five percent for me. And
29   the agency will want their cut. I wonder if God is big
30   enough?
31   RUSH DIPACE: Besides, what's to keep other churches
32   from doing the same thing?
33   EDDIE CATE: You're right. If it worked, other churches
34   might start promoting God as well.

1 **DR. WILL B. KNOWN: We'd never be able to keep it to**
2   **ourselves.**
3 **A. GENT: Well, it was a good idea, but it looks like we're all**
4   **in agreement that there's just not much future in**
5   **promoting God. What other assets does your church**
6   **possess?**
7 **RUSH DIPACE: Well, there is our church softball team. We**
8   **went nine and eight last season.**
9
10
11
12
13
14
15
16
17
18
19
20
21
22
23
24
25
26
27
28
29
30
31
32
33
34

First Church of Reserve

by Robert A. Allen

"Why, some of our best people
wouldn't come if they had to stand
in line with...well, you know."

Is church a place to spread the water of life or to conserve it?

CAST OF CHARACTERS

Fossit Turner

Redd E. Goforth

PROPS

Chair, large spigot (either made of gray cardboard or imaginary), empty bucket.

PRODUCTION NOTES

Fossit Turner is in charge of a very large spigot. His chair is placed right beside it so he can guard it at all times.

1   *(FOSSIT TURNER is sitting in his chair, sound asleep.)*

2   **REDD E. GOFORTH:** *(Enters from left carrying bucket.)* **Hey**
3   **there.**

4   **FOSSIT TURNER:** *(Rubbing his eyes)* **Not so loud! Can't you**
5   **see you're in church?**

6   **REDD E. GOFORTH: I guess I should've known since you**
7   **were sleeping. What church is this?**

8   **FOSSIT TURNER: We call it the First Church of Reserve.**

9   **REDD E. GOFORTH: Great. I see you have just what I need.**

10   **FOSSIT TURNER: Really? What's that?**

11   **REDD E. GOFORTH: A big spigot.**

12   **FOSSIT TURNER: Are you calling me names?**

13   **REDD E. GOFORTH: No. Spigot. A place where you get**
14   **water. A faucet.**

15   **FOSSIT TURNER: Fossit! That's right. Fossit Turner.**

16   *(FOSSIT extends his hand, shaking REDD's.)*

17   **REDD E. GOFORTH: Pleased to meet you. I'm Redd E.**
18   **Goforth.**

19   **FOSSIT TURNER: Welcome to the First Church of**
20   **Reserve. Now what was it you needed?**

21   **REDD E. GOFORTH: Water.**

22   **FOSSIT TURNER: Water?**

23   **REDD E. GOFORTH: Water. If you'll just open that spigot**
24   **and fill this bucket, I'll be on my way.**

25   **FOSSIT TURNER: Now wait just a minute. It's not that**
26   **simple, you know. What are you going to do with this**
27   **water?**

28   **REDD E. GOFORTH: I'm going to give it to my neighbor.**

29   **FOSSIT TURNER: Your neighbor? And what part of town**
30   **do you live in?**

31   **REDD E. GOFORTH: What part of town? What difference**
32   **does that make? My neighbor needs the water.**

33   **FOSSIT TURNER: Well, we've learned from experience**
34   **that if people get water from our church – even if**

1   someone gives it to them, someone like yourself –

2   well, we learned that they usually come back for more.

3   REDD E. GOFORTH: Well, isn't that what you want? Isn't

4   that what the water is for?

5   FOSSIT TURNER: Don't you understand? We can't have

6   just anyone coming here for water. Why, some of our

7   best people wouldn't come if they had to stand in line

8   with...well, you know.

9   REDD E. GOFORTH: So you won't give water to just anybody.

10   FOSSIT TURNER: Oh, you're wrong there. If they come for

11   water, we'll give them water. It's free, you know.

12   REDD E. GOFORTH: I thought it was.

13   FOSSIT TURNER: Of course, we expect them to dress right.

14   REDD E. GOFORTH: Dress right? To get water?

15   FOSSIT TURNER: Sure. Many years ago, some very wise

16   men decided that if you wanted water from the First

17   Church of Reserve, you had to dress right. For

18   example, women have to wear pink polka dots.

19   REDD E. GOFORTH: You don't let women wear blue polka

20   dots?

21   FOSSIT TURNER: Oh, they can wear blue polka dots if

22   they want to, but they have to get their water some-

23   place else.

24   REDD E. GOFORTH: I see. And men?

25   FOSSIT TURNER: No eyeglasses or toupees.

26   REDD E. GOFORTH: But what if they need eyeglasses?

27   FOSSIT TURNER: I didn't start the tradition, I just

28   enforce it.

29   REDD E. GOFORTH: And how do you know if it's a toupee?

30   FOSSIT TURNER: I pull their hair.

31   REDD E. GOFORTH: Every time they come to get water?

32   FOSSIT TURNER: Every time. A guy can lose his hair real

33   fast these days.

34   REDD E. GOFORTH: I'm sure they can around here. Well,

1   I really need that water, so I guess you can pull my
2   hair if you must. Do you suppose you could turn the
3   spigot on now?
4   FOSSIT TURNER: Now? I wouldn't think of it. You'll have
5   to wait until it's time.
6   REDD E. GOFORTH: Until it's time?
7   FOSSIT TURNER: Faucet time. We only give out water
8   once a week, you know. It's really an exciting time.
9   Everyone is standing around with their empty
10   buckets, just waiting for the water to flow. They sing a
11   few songs to get me warmed up, and then I turn the
12   tap and they all fill their buckets. Takes about half an
13   hour, but once in a while we go a few minutes more
14   than that.
15   REDD E. GOFORTH: And one bucket of water lasts them
16   all week?
17   FOSSIT TURNER: Sure. Takes most of the week for it to
18   evaporate.
19   REDD E. GOFORTH: Evaporate?
20   FOSSIT TURNER: Right. They leave their buckets here so
21   they won't forget them the next time they come.
22   Nothing worse than coming to get water without a
23   bucket, is there?
24   REDD E. GOFORTH: I guess not. Unless it's coming to get
25   water when your bucket is already full.
26   FOSSIT TURNER: Yeah, right. That would be bad too. So
27   they leave them here, and by the next week, they're
28   ready to fill them up again.
29   REDD E. GOFORTH: Have you ever thought of just
30   attaching a hose and running the water out to where
31   it's needed?
32   FOSSIT TURNER: Oh, we talked about it once, but cooler
33   heads prevailed.
34   REDD E. GOFORTH: You're not afraid of running out,

1   are you?

2   FOSSIT TURNER: Nope, we have an inexhaustible supply.

3   REDD E. GOFORTH: So what's the problem?

4   FOSSIT TURNER: Well, we've put a lot of money into this
5   spigot, and it has to be maintained. If people come
6   here to get their water, they'll realize that. Besides, if
7   we just let the water run, we won't be able to control
8   where it ends up.

9   REDD E. GOFORTH: You mean, it might find its way to a
10   really dirty area that hasn't had a lot of water?

11   FOSSIT TURNER: Right. We really prefer to see the water
12   used on well-tended gardens which are capable of
13   producing some beautiful fruit. It is so exciting to see
14   beautiful fruit as a result of our efforts to spread the
15   water freely. So will you be back for our service? Our
16   organist is planning to use Handel's *Water Music.*

17   REDD E. GOFORTH: No thanks. I think I'll go to a place
18   where I can get water more frequently. Besides, I can
19   pull out my own hair.

20

21

22

23

24

25

26

27

28

29

30

31

32

33

34

GLOSSARY OF STAGE TERMS

Ad-lib: Dialog not specified in the script but spoken by actors spontaneously, often in crowd scenes.

Adaptation: Changing a previously existing story into dramatic form. If the story is still under copyright, permission to adapt must be obtained.

Antagonist: The character in a play who opposes the protagonist, trying to keep that person from achieving his or her goal.

Arena stage: Also called "theatre in the round." The stage is set in the middle of the room with the audience sitting on all four sides.

Backdrop: A scene painted on canvas, usually hung at the back of a stage set.

Blocking: The movement of actors on-stage, usually determined by a director.

Box set: A stage set with three walls. The fourth wall is imaginary and open to the audience.

Breaking character: To stop acting the role, allowing your own personality to emerge.

Business: Actor's movements smaller than those involved in blocking. Business enhances character development and is usually determined by the actor.

Cast of characters: The list of all the characters involved in a play, usually included at the beginning of a script.

Climax: The pinnacle of the dramatic action; a turning point for good or bad.

Comedy: A broad term used to describe drama where the primary purpose includes effects designed to make the audience laugh.

Conflict: In a playscript, the tension between the protagonist and the antagonist which demands a resolution and thus sets up the action of the play.

Cue: Words or actions that set up an actor's next line.

Dialog: The speeches delivered by the characters in a play.

Downstage: Area toward the front of the stage closest to the audience.

Dramatic action: Action planned by the playwright to create atmosphere, reveal character and advance the plot line.

London format: A common organizational arrangement for playscripts with the character names in the left-hand column.

Mime: Also "pantomime." Using action and gesture to tell a story without words.

Motivation: An actor's reasons for actions or dialog.

New York format: A common organizational arrangement for playscripts with the character names in the middle of the page.

Off-stage: The stage area which cannot be seen by the audience.

On-stage: The stage area which can be seen by the audience.

Plot: In a playscript, the development of the events of the drama.

Properties: Also "props." Items used by actors on-stage.

Proscenium: An opening, usually hung with a curtain, which separates the stage from the audience, creating a frame around the stage.

Protagonist: The main character, the one who starts the action of the play and tries to achieve its main goal.

Readers Theatre: A style of dramatic presentation which emphasizes the script, usually characterized by a group interpretive approach to literature.

Realism: A dramatic technique which seeks to represent life as it really exists.

Resolution: In a playscript, the events which resolve the conflict of the play.

Royalty: A sum paid to the playwright or publisher for permission to present a play.

Secondary roles: Members of the cast who figure prominently in the story, though not as heavily as the protagonist and antagonist.

Scene: The place where the play happens. Could also refer to part of an act, as in "Scene One."

Skrim: An opaque curtain which becomes transparent when lit from behind.

Sketch: A short play with a purpose. Seeks to make a point rather than just entertain.

Skit: A short play whose only purpose is to entertain an audience.

Special effects: Unusual visual or auditory techniques designed to create atmosphere for a play.

Stage curtain: The curtain separating the stage from the audience in a proscenium stage.

Stage left: The area to the actor's left as he faces the audience.

Stage right: The area to the actor's right as he faces the audience.

Symbolism: A dramatic technique which seeks to present life through metaphorical or symbolic means.

Technical action: Actions planned by the director, such as entrances and exits.

Tour: A series of performances in different places by an acting troupe.

Theatre-in-the-round: Also "arena stage." The stage is set in the middle of the room with the audience on all four sides.

Theme: The attitude toward the subject of the play, chosen by the playwright.

Thrust stage: A stage which extends into an auditorium with audience seated on three sides.

Troupe: A group of actors who work together on a variety of productions.

Upstage: Area away from the audience toward the backstage wall.

BIBLIOGRAPHY

Albright, Hardie and Anita Albright. *Acting: The Creative Process.* Belmont, California: Wadsworth Publishing Company, 1980.

Barranger, Milly S. *Theatre: A Way of Seeing.* Belmont, California: Wadsworth Publishing Company, 1986.

Bennett, Gordon C. *Readers Theatre Comes to Church.* Colorado Springs, Colorado: Meriwether Publishing, Ltd., 1985.

Card, Orson Scott. *Characters and Viewpoint.* Cincinnati, Ohio: Writer's Digest Books, 1988.

Catron, Louis E. *The Director's Vision.* Mountain View, California: Mayfield Publishing, 1989.

Coger, Leslie A. and Melvin R. White. *Readers Theatre Handbook.* Glenview, Illinois: Scott, Foresman and Company, 1973.

Hull, Raymond. *How to Write a Play.* Cincinnati, Ohio: Writer's Digest Books, 1983.

McGaw, Charles and Larry D. Clark. *Acting Is Believing.* Fort Worth, Texas: Harcourt Brace Jovanovich, 1992.

Miller, J. William. *Modern Playwrights at Work.* New York, NY: Samuel French, Inc., 1968.

Shamus, Laura. *Playwriting for Theatre, Film and Television:* White Hall, Virginia: Betterway Publications, 1991.

Smiley, Sam. *Playwriting: The Structure of Action.* Englewood Cliffs, New Jersey: Prentice-Hall, 1971.

ABOUT THE AUTHOR

© 1995 Guy Cali Assoc.

Robert Allen plays the roles of husband, father and teacher in Clarks Summit, Pennsylvania. The supporting cast includes his wife, Carmen, and their five children — four in their twenty-somethings and a five-year-old tagalong. His plays have often been performed by the Pillsbury Players, whom he directed for eight years. He now directs the Pastoral Ministry program at Baptist Bible College of Pennsylvania, training ministers to add drama to their preaching. Previous roles have included the pastorate, camp evangelist and teaching college drama and communications courses; experiences which provided the background for the writing of *Don't Give Up the Script.*

ORDER FORM

MERIWETHER PUBLISHING LTD.
P.O. BOX 7710
COLORADO SPRINGS, CO 80933
TELEPHONE: (719) 594-4422

Please send me the following books:

_____	**Don't Give Up the Script #CC-B204**	**$12.95**

by **Robert A. Allen**
Writing original sketches for the church

_____ **Divine Comedies #CC-B190**   **$12.95**
by **T. M. Williams**
A collection of plays for church drama groups

_____ **Sermons Alive! #CC-B132**   **$12.95**
by **Paul Neale Lessard**
52 dramatic sketches for worship services

_____ **Get a Grip! #CC-B128**   **$10.95**
by **L. G. Enscoe and Annie Enscoe**
Contemporary scenes and monologs for Christian teens

_____ **The Best of the Jeremiah People #CC-B117**   **$14.95**
by **Jim Custer and Bob Hoose**
Humorous skits and sketches by leading Christian repertory group

_____ **Fool of the Kingdom #CC-B202·**   **$12.95**
by **Philip D. Noble**
How to be an effectice clown minister

_____ **Christmas on Stage #CC-B153**   **$15.95**
by **Theodore O. Zapel**
An anthology of Christmas plays for performance

These and other fine Meriwether Publishing books are available at your local Christian bookstore or direct from the publisher. Use the handy order form on this page.

NAME: _____

ORGANIZATION NAME: _____

ADDRESS: _____

CITY: _____ STATE: _____

ZIP: _____ PHONE: _____

❑ **Check Enclosed**
❑ **Visa or MasterCard #** _____

                        Expiration
Signature: _____ *Date:* _____
       (required for Visa/MasterCard orders)

COLORADO RESIDENTS: Please add 3% sales tax.
SHIPPING: Include $2.75 for the first book and 50¢ for each additional book ordered.

❑ *Please send me a copy of your complete catalog of books and plays.*